JUST WE TWO

Life From a Feline Perspective

By

Lindy Carandell

supervising (safely from the closet)!

On our third full day there, a big truck came and several men brought in our furniture and lots of boxes. I didn't actually see them, as Cherokee talked me into hiding with him, but it was noisy and kind of scary with all those strange people in the house. By the afternoon, they were done, and they left. We now had the couch, the chairs, the tables, and the bed. All Mom's clothes were in a big box and it took her a while to put them all away in the closet. We came out later, when she was done working and it was time for our supper. It was an exciting day, and we were all very tired and slept well, after Mom made the bed. No more sleeping on the thing on the floor.

Before long, some more furniture came, brought by more men. There was something to put the TV on (the TV from home) and a place to put the good dishes. Most of the rest of the next several days were spent in the garage, unpacking boxes and putting stuff away. It was very hot, and when Mom had the big garage door open, we couldn't go out with her. She was always worried that we would go away. Fat chance of that! We liked to explore, but we would never forget to come home for supper!

Sometimes, Mom let us go out onto what she called the patio. It had a high wall around it and had some bushy stuff and some weeds growing in it. It was fun, though. There were some little creatures that were kind of green or brown and they ran on the walls. What fun to chase them and catch them! Cherokee didn't catch any - he always left that to me. I would catch them and we both would play with them. Sometimes their tails came off and would lie there wiggling.

That really freaked Mom out when she found one on the hall floor - a wiggling tail, I mean. She called these creatures geckos.

After a few days, some people came to stay for a couple of days. They slept on the futon in the guest room. I guess maybe they were guests. They stayed a couple of nights and then left. Mom seemed happy to see them, but they took her away for most of one day. Anyway, we weren't so happy to see them and were glad when they left. Mom said that they were relatives, her niece and her husband and that she had been happy to see them. That's two nieces. What are nieces, anyway? I don't think I have any nieces, and Cherokee didn't think he had any either.

Oh, ya-a-a-a-awn! This has really tired me out.

Yours,
Apache

More Happy Home

Good morning! Or is it afternoon? Or even evening? Just up from my latest nap. Yawn!

I need to address why I call Cherokee disgusting. Before we moved to the house called Phoenix, he was always congested and stuffy. He sneezed constantly. Mom said he had allergies or maybe even asthma. Sometimes when he would sneeze, stuff (Mom calls it snot) would come out of his nose and hang there. He would go all over the house with that stuff hanging off his nose. Mom would try to wipe it off, but he would never let her and would struggle mightily if she tried. Did he think she was trying to smother him, or what? Anyway, it was perfectly disgusting! After our move, he stopped his constant sneezing and usually then it happened only when it rained. Mom was happy that he was better. She was also better, because she had pretty much the same problem, except that she would wipe her nose. She would even blow the stuff out before it had a chance to hang out. She has much better habits than Cherokee ever did.

I believe I told you before about one of his litter box habits. Totally disgusting! Mom said that he was a man, what could we expect. I think for some reason she has changed her attitude since then, though. I just looked back and found that I did not mention his bad habit of leaving something extremely smelly in the litter box and not covering it up. Even Mom could smell it and if she wasn't around to cover it up, I would have to go into the box and cover it very well myself.

Cherokee also loved to wrestle. I believe that I mentioned before that he was always bothering me during my nap times, because he wanted to play and/or wrestle. Often I would get very angry and we would end up fighting instead, leaving more big clumps of fur for Mom to find. She used to worry that we would really hurt each other sometime, but it didn't happen. We were pretty easy on each other, even though we would hiss (mostly I would) and growl (mostly I would) while rolling around on the floor or the furniture. It scared Mom, and I'm sorry that it did, but what could I do?

I don't remember a whole lot about our time in Malden, since one day seemed to be very much like the previous one. Here in Phoenix, though, I remember most of our time. In some ways it is a more interesting house than Malden, because there are steps. However, there were a lot more windows and a lot more to see in the old place, although there wasn't much place to sit by the window in the winter, when they were closed. Here we have window sills big enough to get on, even when the windows are shut. There just isn't much to see. From the patio doors we can see the patio and sometimes a bird or a butterfly, but mostly just the high wall. From the eating room window, we can't see much at all, just the plants growing along the front walk, and another high wall. From the bedroom window, again, not much to see, except a little bit into the car place and the garage roof. From the office window, we can see into a few other peoples' patios and see more birds and butterflies, so that is the best window in the house, in my opinion. However, it is very hot there on a sunny day.

Cherokee always liked to be in the eating room

window, because he could see plants, bees, birds, butterflies, etc. He would sit there for hours at a time. Sometimes I would go up there, too. It was harder for me than for Cherokee, because he was always a better jumper than I.

Well, I'm a little tired right now, and I can't think of the rest of Cherokee's disgusting habits, so I will leave you now so that I can meditate and think about things, about life, about the past. I'll get to the present soon enough, but I'll leave that for another day.

Yours,
Apache

Another Move

Today I have not napped so much. Mom has had some problems to take care of and with all her moving around and talking on the phone, I find that it is difficult to sleep. It's very inconsiderate of her.

I must address our next move at this time. When we came to Phoenix, Mom was renting our house and after a while, Uncle Sam kept needing too much money, so she bought a house. I'm not sure why buying a house would mean she had to send less money to her uncle, but that's what she said. Maybe he felt sorry for us for having to spend more money. Anyway, she bought the house next door to where we were living. When she started putting stuff in boxes, I thought that maybe we were in for another long trip in the car in our boxes. Thank heavens I was wrong (for the first time). She even had a couple of people come to help her with the boxes. They took them out of the house, but didn't bring anything back.

Before many days went by, a couple of men came and started taking out the furniture. Cherokee and I were shut in the guest room in our boxes. It was a frightening experience. We didn't know what was happening or where we were going. As long as it wasn't the vet, though, I guess it was okay. Anyway, finally Mom took our boxes and we thought we were going to the car, but she just walked a little way and into another house. She put us in what turned out to be the guest room in the new house. The futon was all set up again, and the bookcases were there, although there weren't any books in them. She let us out of our boxes and shut the door. We were in the room with our food, water, and litter box, so it wasn't too bad. We could hear the men in the other room, and at one point, we saw them on the patio, handing the patio furniture from the old house over the wall to the new one.

While we were shut in the guest room, someone came to visit. It was the woman who had watched over us while Mom was gone a couple of times. She brought someone else with her to meet us. Well, they got to meet me, but it took them quite a while to find Cherokee. Mind you, the closet was closed, so he couldn't go up on the top shelf and hide. They looked under and behind the futon, but he wasn't there. Mom was starting to get a little worried, even though she knew he had to be in that room. At last she looked up on top of one of the bookcases and there he was, lying as flat as he could, so no one could see him from the floor. They laughed about it and wondered how he got up there, as those bookcases are pretty high. I will never tell, though.

The futon is very nice. Cherokee and I like it a lot. On the bottom part, there is a mattress and most of the time it is a couch, but when those guests came to visit, it turned into a bed. Over that, there is another, smaller bed. It also has a mattress, and I must say that it is very comfortable. Cherokee and I spend quite a bit of nap time on it.

It took a while, but finally the new house began to seem like home. The couch room was smaller, so the big, sectional couch didn't fit in very well. Also, the coffee table and end table were too large and you could hardly walk between the coffee table and the TV holder to get to the patio doors. Other than that, I couldn't see much difference between the old house and the new house, except that everything seemed to be turned around. Mom didn't like the closet in the food room, so one day she took out the three shelves that were in the closet and replaced them with four shelves. What a lot of noise! Sawing and hammering! She seemed to be happy after that, and she put a lot of stuff away in that closet.

There was not as much sun in the new house, but Cherokee still loved the eating room window, maybe even more, because the new house is where the vines grew over the window when Mom let them. The vines had a very fitting name - cat's claw! I like that. Cherokee said that the vines made him feel as though he were hiding in the bushes, because the birds and butterflies could not see him. He just wished that he could be really hiding in real bushes so he could hunt those creatures. Ha! He was never a hunter! If there was any hunting to be done, I always had to do it.

Pretty soon, things calmed down and were more or less back to normal. We got our breakfast in the morning before Mom went to work, and we got our supper when she came home. It was a good quiet life for the most part, until Mom decided to start having parties. More on that later. I'm tired now, and must take a nap.

Yours,
Apache

Odd Customs

Yawn, yawn, yawn! Nothing like a good stretch after a nap!

I was just thinking today about some odd customs I have noticed. One of the oddest is during the early part of each year (when the days are at their darkest), when Mom talks about her Uncle Sam a lot. I have met some of her relatives like nieces, daughter, grandson, sister, brother, even cousins, but never this Uncle Sam. I didn't know she had one, but she must, and he must be very poor, because she sends him a lot of money each year. We certainly are not rich, and sometimes Mom will wonder aloud where my next meal is coming from. Horrors! I could starve! Well, I haven't yet. Actually, Mom takes very good care of us and we always have good food to eat. As long as I have enough to eat, all is well. As it is, Mom could stand to eat a little less.

Another odd custom was when Cherokee would put his dry food into the water dish. It turned the water brown and made it most unappetizing looking. Since it was food flavored, I could drink it, but just barely. Mom didn't like it either. She said it stained the dish and she would have to scrub it out. After he would let the food soak in the water for a while, he would take it out with his paws and eat it. Then he would shake his legs and paws to get the water off and would leave water drops all over everything and puddles on the floor. At first Mom thought he was getting his paws wet in the litter box and was incredibly disgusted when she found footprints on the table. Finally she realized that it was from the water dish and not the litter box and felt a lot better about it. It's not that she allowed him up on the table, because she didn't. Of course, he went up there anyway and got down only when she saw him and made him get down.

Cherokee also had the custom of looking out of every window and door he could reach, which is to say all of them. We have a very high, yellow-colored, arched window in the stairwell. It is up near the second floor ceiling, with no access whatsoever. It does not open. I know this because Cherokee often would get up on the half-wall at the top of the steps and jump over to that window. It is a very small, narrow place, but he was determined. I'm not sure why, since you can't see out of it because of the pattern and the color. Whatever made him happy! When Mom would see him jump over there, it was all she could do to keep from screaming, she was so afraid for him. She did not scream, though, because she knew it would startle him and maybe make him fall. Also, she would be holding her breath, so she couldn't scream anyway. She is a very good Mom that way, always concerned for our safety.

Mom also has the custom of bringing a tree into the house every year. I find it very strange, but it does smell rather nice, like the outdoors. She sets it up in a container of water and then puts lights and sparkly things on it. I guess it looks nice, and Mom likes it a lot. After it has been up for a while, she puts presents on the white sheet that is under it. Some of the presents are for us. The only presents I really like, though, are the food ones, like tuna and salmon. And also treats, yummy, crunchy treats! Um-m-m-m-m! She talks about someone named Santa Claus. Who is this? Another mysterious relative? Supposedly he brings the presents, but I've never seen him, and I have watched. This last year, Mom did not put up a tree. She was afraid that Pest would climb it and ruin things. She was probably right!

Other customs are called holidays. For instance, the tree is put up for the Christmas holiday, and she cooks a prime rib roast. Yum! Yum! When I first came to live with Mom, it took me a while to acquire a taste for beef, but now I think it's pretty darned good. Then there is Easter, when she cooks lamb. O-o-o-o-o-h! I love lamb! Very yummy! She usually boils eggs and colors them, too. The eggs are okay, but I much prefer the lamb. On the holiday called Thanksgiving, she cooks a turkey and I am in seventh heaven! I think bird is my favorite food. One day I was out on the patio, and a bird came within reach. I quickly swiped at it and brought it down onto the bricks of the patio. I was about to bite into a lovely meal of bird, when Mom came out and made me let go. The bird crawled under the grill and by the next day, he was gone. I know, I looked. I guess Mom has never caught and eaten a bird before. If she had, she would realize just how great fresh bird is.

Well, there are probably other customs that I haven't thought of, but talking about all this eating and jumping around has made me very tired. So, for safety's sake, I will go to my bed and nap for a while.

Yours,
Apache

Did I Say Quiet Life?

Is it time to wake up already? It seems as though I only just lay down for a nap.

In my last post, I said that life was quiet until Mom decided to start giving parties. About a year after the move to the new place, Mom decided that she needed some life in her life, so to speak. She had been meeting people (men) for some time and going out with them. Most of them never got to first base with me, because I didn't care to come out from under the bed where Cherokee and I always went when people came over. She decided that she would give a Post-Holiday Blues party in January. She said that many people fall into a sort of depression after the holidays and can be cheered up with a party. Looking around the house, she felt that our furniture had to go. She still had that nasty, big sectional in the little, bitty couch room. It was not very clean and it smelled bad.

One day, some men came in a truck and brought in a couch, two end tables, a table and chairs for the eating room, and a couch for the guest room. All the old stuff was put into the garage. The new couch was brown and covered in a material that I don't like the feel of (Mom calls it microfiber). It's good enough for scratching, but I don't like to lie on it. When Mom saw that Cherokee and I were scratching it, she covered it with quilts. Then it was good to lie on. The couch has a long cushion at one end and Mom likes to lie on that to watch TV. She calls that long cushion a "chase." I can't think why it is called a chase, since it just sits there and doesn't chase anything or anyone, and nothing chases it. How to explain human things? We are always happy, though, to join her and help her be comfortable when she sits on it.

We later found out that the couch in the guest room can turn into a bed. Very interesting! However, it was almost always just a couch. The eating room table and chairs were very nice and went well with the dish keeper she bought when we moved out here. The end tables were okay, I guess. Mom still was not quite satisfied, and a short time later, she brought home a big, new TV. The old one no longer worked and she had brought the little TV down from her bedroom. The new one had a flat screen and it was one that Mom could lift by herself. She was still not satisfied, and then the comfy chair entered our lives. This is a chair that Mom can almost lie down in, or sit up in. She calls it a recliner. Again, I don't like the material, but with the quilt on it, it is fine. When Mom sits in the comfy chair, she puts the quilt over her lap and legs, reclines, and then we join her. What a wonderful invention. I thoroughly approve of this kind of chair. We could lie there for hours, the three of us. One more thing was needed to complete the furnishings, though. We had no coffee table. Mom looked for a long time and, finally, she came home with a set of three of what she called nesting tables. Each one is pretty small, but they take up very little room, and give people places to set things on when they are un-nested.

Well, we were finally ready for a party. E-mail announcements went out to lots of people and Mom was all excited when the day came. She had a little help preparing, but she was still really tired when it was all over. Anyway, there was lots of great-smelling food (we could smell it even under the bed) and lots of people. Mom said later that someone had counted about 150 people altogether over the duration of the party. She said it was a great success. I don't actually agree with that, but that's my opinion. Once it got pretty late and most of the people were gone, hunger drove Cherokee and me downstairs. People oohed and aawed over me, but I concentrated on trying to get Mom's attention for our supper. Stupid Cherokee saw someone sitting in the comfy chair and, thinking that it was Mom, he jumped right up into a stranger's lap. He wasn't sure what to do when he realized it wasn't Mom, but the stranger began to pet him, so he stayed for a little while. Mom finally got the idea that we needed our supper.

The next day was devoted to cleaning up. What a mess! There wasn't much meat left, mostly vegetables and other inedibles, but Mom had saved us a little bit of good stuff. I was glad that the party was over. Now life could settle down again. Mom had other ideas, though. In April, she decided to have another party. It was called Spring Fling. She had the patio and the garage roof ready for people, as well as the inside of the house. This time, all of the old furniture was gone from the garage, and she put the food tables out there. She cooked a lot of good meat for the party, and she saved some for us. Maybe parties aren't all that bad, after all! Again, she said it was a success and decided to have another party in June, but out at the community pool this time. Cherokee and I weren't bothered much by that party, thank goodness, but we also didn't get much to eat from it.

Wow! A lot of parties, but she didn't have another one until the following January, and then another one in April after that. Right around the time of the April party, Mom started being gone a lot more. She said she got a second job.

That meant that she left the house around 7:30 in the morning for her first job, then worked all afternoon and evening at her second job, getting home around 9:30 at night. I didn't like that one bit. That was a very long time to wait for food! Most inconsiderate of her! She kept telling us that we wouldn't have anything to eat if she didn't work the second job, so I guess it was okay. It was still an awful long time between breakfast and supper, though.

Mom didn't have another party until the next April, after she had been working the second job for a year. Again, lots of good meat to eat! I think maybe I could get used to parties, after all. After that party, however, our lives changed once again.

Well, all this thinking about food has made me sleepy so I will adjourn to my bed so I can sleep and can dream about fresh bird and other fine foods. Ya-a-a-awn! Later!

Yours,
Apache

Ruminations

Well, it's dark outside, and I'm done napping for a while. I had a good rest, thank you.

I've been thinking a lot lately and many ideas have been running around in my head. I mentioned fresh bird before, and I would like to expand on that. Catching birds is not necessarily about eating, although if you live in the wild it is. I like to catch them because they make me angry! They are very annoying, especially those little buzz birds, or maybe they are big bugs even. Mom says they are called hummingbirds, but I call them buzz birds. When I am outside on the patio, they buzz my head constantly and I just hate that buzzing sound. They are always just beyond my reach, and very fast. I'm pretty fast myself, but they are really fast. Mom says they are not big enough to even be a snack for me, but I don't care. I would just like to stop that buzzing. Other birds, that I haven't even seen, make me crazy, too. One makes sort of a squawking sound. Mom likes it - says it sounds a little like a parrot, and says they are called boat-tailed grackles. I would like to catch them, too. Sometimes I hear those crazy doves all day long. O-o-oh what I would like to do to them to make them stop that constant cooing noise! Mom says they are called Inca doves. Finally, there is what Mom calls the mockingbird. A very hateful bird! Sometimes they even sing at night! They sing very loud and sing lots of different songs. They sound really meaty, though! Mom loves them all and tries to get me to see their good sides, but I would catch and eat them all if I could.

Cherokee loved to sit on the window sill behind the cat's claw vines and watch the little buzz birds. He was just fascinated by them and was not particularly interested in catching one. He always left the hunting to me. When I would bring one of the little, icky green things that Mom calls geckos into the house, he was always happy to play with it or its tail, but he just was not into catching anything, only playing. I do love to go out onto the patio and catch things. There are the loud, black bugs that Mom says are called crickets. What fun! Also, one time I caught a grasshopper (at least that's what Mom called it). They hop around all kinds of ways and present a real challenge to my hunting skills. I love it!

One time, Mom let us out onto the patio in the morning, before she left for work. It was cool and nice out there and it was a great day for exploring. Mom never let us go up on the wall (if she saw us, that is), but I felt it was worth taking a chance on that particular day. I went a long way down the wall and saw into all sorts of houses and patios. I heard Mom calling us to go back into the house, but I just didn't feel like it. Things were much too interesting up on the wall. Later on, when I was done looking around, I went back to our patio, but found the door closed and locked. What a shock! What was I going to do? No food, no water, no comfy bed or chair to lie on. I found a shady place and I lay down on the bricks and just waited for Mom to open the door. Well, she didn't open the door until she got home from wherever it was she went. She was angry to find me out there, because she thought I had come into the house before she called and had been hiding under the bed. She scolded me, and it was quite a while before we were let out again. I don't think she ever let us go out by ourselves again. Sometimes Cherokee would jump up on the wall, but he was too chicken to go anywhere, and Mom would yell at him and he would immediately jump down and go back into the house.

There were a lot of strange felines in the neighborhood. I met some of them on my sojourn that day that I went down the wall. They told me that they lived outside in a colony and that I would be welcome to join them. It seemed very tempting at first, but then I remembered the nice, soft furniture that I would lie on and the delicious food that Mom served. I decided that it was best to go home. My wild life had been left behind long before and probably it was best to leave it that way. I had also heard that there were some scary things out there - owls, hawks, and eagles, and coyotes (I think this is a kind of dog). If I lived outside with the wild felines, there would be a lot of danger, and I didn't think I wanted that. Safety, a soft bed, good food served to me, a brother to play with, a mom to cuddle with - what more could I want?

All I can say is: life happens. And much of it did. There are so many changes that we have to face, some of them life-altering. I always try to put on my happy face and move on, even though sometimes it's very, very hard to do.

Mom is going to bed now, so I think I will go with her. It's so soft and warm in the bed with her and it's so nice, especially when Pest leaves us alone. Good night!

Yours,
Apache

A New Housemate

Kitta

I just woke up! What a wonderful nap. Ya-a-a-wn!

In this post I wish to tell you about a very unhappy person. One day, a man came over and brought in some boxes and took them up to Mom's office. He was up there for a while and they talked quite a bit, then he left. He didn't take the boxes with him. Cherokee and I were, of course, curious as to what the man had brought into our house. Mom kept the door shut for a while, but then she let us see later on. For goodness sake! It was an all-black feline. As we got to know her over the following days and weeks, we found that she was an older female who was quite cranky. She had been with the man for some time and she was very angry that suddenly she found herself at our house, with us, torn away from her Dad. She told us that some of her ancestors were from Siam, and that made her special. We didn't quite see it that way, though.

She was very snooty and bragged about her electric litter box. We found it rather scary and smelly. When Mom would clean out the collection container, there would be litter on the carpet underneath. Also, some of the stuff she left in there got stuck on the mechanisms and had to be specially cleaned off. She came to us without a name (I think she had been called "Cat," so Mom meditated on it for a while and realized that her name was Kitta. Not a bad name, if you ask me, but no one did. Kitta didn't care too much for it, but then she didn't care too much for anything, except trying to figure out how to get back to her Daddy.

As I said before, Kitta was elderly, and sometimes she didn't always get everything into the litter box, and the office began to smell. Evidently, she had peed a lot off the side of the box and the carpet was in very bad shape. Mom really didn't know what to do about her. She took Kitta in so that the man would not take her to be euthanized. That's what they would have done because of her age. Probably no one would have adopted her. We felt a little sorry for Kitta, and wanted to get to know her and maybe even cuddle with her, but she was not open to that sort of thing, preferring to stay aloof. Mom moved her down to the guest room, and sometimes would let her out into the rest of the house, but she would just attack us. She was not gentle and used her claws and teeth to their fullest. Eventually, we decided that we didn't like her and didn't want her in our house anymore, but what could we do?

One day, Mom was petting Kitta and trying to get her to be affectionate, but mostly she scratched and bit Mom, too. Well, Mom found a lump in Kitta's side. Into the box and off to the vet she went. As Mom told it, the vet was going to do a biopsy (whatever that is), but in feeling the lump realized that it was something called a hernia, so Mom said to go ahead and fix it. Expensive! Kitta came home extra-grouchy and wearing what Mom called an Elizabethan collar. How funny! Cherokee and I laughed like crazy when we would see her. She hated the collar, she hated the vet, she hated Mom, she hated us. So much anger in one small, black-furred body!

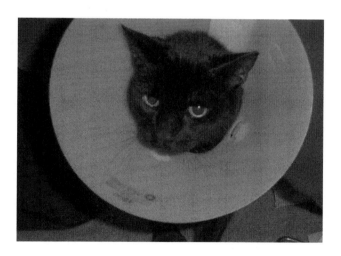

Kitta in her Elizabethan Collar

Some time later, Mom realized that Kitta was missing the litter box most of the time and had thoroughly ruined the carpet in the guest room. Realizing that there was probably something more wrong with Kitta, back to the vet they went. Kitta did not come back. Mom said that the vet felt she was very old and quite sick and that she would probably never be in really good health, having either kidney failure or diabetes. Not long after that, Mom ripped up the carpet in the guest room, with the help of a friend. The concrete slab underneath even smelled bad. She scrubbed it and put all kinds of things on it to make the smell go away. Eventually it did. However, the little bit of carpet left in the office still gives off an odor sometimes, especially on humid days.

Cherokee and I were not sorry to see Kitta gone. She was just making our lives miserable. I'm sorry that her end had to come in such a way, but we definitely did not miss her. Even Mom felt relief. Finally, we could get back to normal.

I hear a nap calling me now, so I need to go answer it. I'm just exhausted thinking about Kitta. I will take a good nap and sleep the thoughts of her right out of my mind.

Yours,
Apache

A Big Surprise

A lovely nap! It's so nice when Mom has the ceiling fan on when it's so hot. I can lie on the cool tile and feel a little breeze blow gently over me. It never fails to put me to sleep.

I think I mentioned before that Mom did a lot of searching online. She is pretty good at it. After all, that's where she found me! She looked at the Humane Society web page when she was in Malden, and when she saw my picture, it was love at first sight. She said I was the most beautiful feline she had ever seen. How right she was!

Anyway, Mom continued online to find a companion for herself. She had mentioned that she used to have a mate, but that they got divorced. When we moved out here to Phoenix, she really knew almost no one. Gradually, she got to know some people - how else could she throw a party? Well, she met a number of different men who, for one reason or another, just were not suitable for her. Cherokee and I knew long before she did, of course, because the smell wasn't right or they obviously didn't like us. While she was still working so much, she decided to have another party. She cleaned the house from top to bottom, using that awful thing, the vacuum cleaner. How we hate that! We always adjourn to the bedroom and under the bed when she uses it. There was a lot of other cleaning to be done, as well. Some time while she was cleaning, she started feeling a pain and had to sit down a lot. The party was good, but she was glad when it was over so she could just rest and try to get rid of that pain.

The pain kept up (she still has it, but is going somewhere to work on it), but after a week or so, she left us alone and the neighbor came in to feed us and clean our litter box. Mom was gone for about four or five days (I was never real good with numbers and time) and what a surprise when she came home! She had someone with her - a man! It was late at night when they got home and after eating a little something, they went right to bed. The next day, we checked him out a little, but we were leery of getting too close. It wasn't long before we decided that he was okay. He smelled okay in a human sort of way and he was very nice to us. Mom kept saying that she brought us a daddy. Whatever that was! (Didn't Kitta say something about a daddy?) Before long, they got married and we realized just what a daddy was. He was very good to us and would slip us treats sometimes when Mom wasn't looking. Now we had a companion, too. He was home with us all day while Mom was off working. He spent a lot of time on the computer, trying to find a way to make money for us, but he would cuddle with us, too. He played with Cherokee sometimes, as well. Mom wasn't real fond of playing, like me, so it was a real treat for Cherokee.

We really liked having Dad around. He cooked food for Mom, he fed us and cleaned our litter box and just plain filled our days with companionship. We now had two people to love, and we did. What a nice family we now had! I am still wondering about one thing, though. Mom says that Dad is from a turkey. What? Do turkeys give birth to humans? I don't really understand that at all. It seems very strange to me. I have never actually seen a baby human. Are there such things? Also, I have never actually seen a living turkey, only a roasted one on a serving platter (that's the best way to see them, in my opinion). So, how does one get a human from a turkey? I had always assumed that baby humans looked just like adult humans, just smaller. Oh well, how does one begin to understand the human mystery?

All of this thinking is making me very tired today. I think I must go take a luscious nap.

Yours,
Apache

My Brother

What a great nap! Time to get up off the couch and eat something.

Sometimes in the past, Cherokee had startled Mom considerably. He rarely said anything - he was the strong and silent type. Once in a while, though, he would do what surprised Mom so much. He would speak the old language from back in the wild woods. Mom described it as sort of like "eh, ih, ah," a very choppy sort of sound, repeated many times. She thought maybe he was trying to speak her language and was maybe practicing his sounds. She didn't know it was the old language. I never really learned it, because I was busy learning to hunt, while Cherokee had lots of time to play and contemplate and learn different things. Mom looked up Maine Coon felines online (because some of our ancestors were Maine Coon) and found that they sometimes spoke the old language. After that, she really liked to hear it, but, as I said, he rarely spoke anything, let alone the old language. No one around him understood it anyway. Cherokee never really developed that connection with Mom that I had, although he completely adored her and would do just about anything she asked.

Cherokee was not as good as I was, though. He often would get into trouble. Food was his passion, and he particularly loved human food. As I have said before, he could jump very well and often jumped up onto the food room counters, looking for the remains of food left in pans on the stove or hoping to find food in the sink that had, unfortunately for him, already been pushed down into the garbage grinder. Mom liked to leave the butter out so it would be soft. Once in a while she would forget to cover it and would come back to find tongue prints in the butter. She would then throw it away, wash the butter dish, and get out some new butter and be careful to cover it all the time. What a guy! I was never into jumping all that much. I was fast on my feet, but I didn't care too much for jumping, especially as I got a little older. It just seemed a little childish. I had everything I needed within reach, why did I need to jump anywhere?

Another thing that Cherokee often did was get Mom up for breakfast. As I said, food was his passion and he had a hard time waiting for breakfast. So, when it got to be light, even just a little bit, he would decide that it was time Mom got up to feed us. He would go upstairs, make a running start into the bedroom and leap on the bed and Mom's stomach as hard as he could. That sure woke her up, let me tell you! She was usually so startled that she didn't have time to get mad at him. Sometimes, she would shut us out of the bedroom after that, but most of the time she would get up and feed us, just as Cherokee wanted.

My brother was not too picky about grooming himself, but he liked to try to do some grooming on Mom. Sometimes he would lick her hair and maybe try to pull some out. He didn't seem to realize that she doesn't shed as much as we do and she usually didn't have any knots in her hair. I think it's kind of funny that she has hair only on her head! What kind of silly idea is that? She has some hair on other parts of her body, but it's very short and very light-colored so you almost can't even see it. Cherokee also liked to try to pull off Mom's fingernails and toenails. At least that's what she said. Actually, he was trying to pull off the claw sheaths, like the ones we have. I guess he never knew that she doesn't have any. He would grip one of her nails in his teeth and pull away. Mom said it didn't really hurt, but she found it very odd of him to do that.

Well, my memory's getting sore and I think I must take a nap to cure that. It's a wonderful day for a nap!

Yours,
Apache

No More Happy Family

At some point after Dad came to live with us, Cherokee told me that he was not feeling very good. He begged me not to tell Mom that he was sick, and he continued to play and jump and be his normal self. He did sleep more, and I tried to help him get better. He pretty much stopped eating after a while and I ate his food so that Mom wouldn't know that he was sick. One evening, he ate something and just couldn't hold it in. He did what Mom called projectile vomiting and it all came up. She was very scared and upset. The next day she put him in the box and took him to the vet. I was afraid that I would never see him again, but she and Dad brought him home again, although he was terribly sick and wouldn't, or couldn't, eat. Mom cried a lot and tried to comfort Cherokee. She tried again to give him something to eat, but it came right up.

One night, Mom and Dad went to bed, leaving Cherokee sleeping on a blanket downstairs. During the night, he crawled upstairs and went into the closet. Mom found him in the morning and he was so very sick. He had left a little blood on the carpet and he was moaning. I felt so helpless! What could I do? Dad picked him up and brought him to Mom, who was sitting in the comfy chair with a towel on her lap. Cherokee just lay there moaning, while Mom and Dad petted him and tried to comfort him, all the while crying themselves. After a little while, they wrapped him in the towel and took him away. I was very scared.

Later on, they came home and laid the towel down on the floor. Something black and white that looked like Cherokee was lying very still on it. I sniffed at it and it had a little smell of Cherokee, but it also smelled of vomit, the vet, and some strange things that I couldn't identify. It lay very still and did not breathe. Dad went out on the patio with a shovel and some other tools. He lifted up some bricks and started digging in the ground underneath. Mom took the black and white thing into the bathroom, put some warm water in the tub and put the thing in. She washed it carefully, as it had vomit on it, then dried it off. She put some smelly oils on it, wrapped it in a white cloth and took it outside. Unfortunately, she had to go off to work, but Dad put the thing in the hole and covered it up. He said a prayer for it.

Where, oh where, was Cherokee? I was so upset and confused. I thought maybe he could explain things to me. I couldn't find him anywhere. Finally, I went to sleep and I slept a lot after that.

I'm a little upset right now, as memories have overwhelmed me. I must take a very long nap.

Yours,
Apache

OMG!!!

Mina

What a long nap! I guess I really needed it. Ya-a-a-awn!

Where, oh where, was Cherokee! I looked high and I looked low. He was nowhere to be found. He wasn't hiding in a closet, and he wasn't hiding under the bed. I kept thinking that at any time Mom would walk through the door carrying the box with Cherokee in it. I called out for him for a long time. Mom tried to comfort me, but it just wasn't much use. My brother was missing and I was missing him! Look, Apache, look! Maybe you missed a place. He's playing a cruel trick on you by hiding somewhere really hard to find. Cherokee! You can come out now. You win!

In my head I knew that he was dead. Mom kept telling me so. She said that she missed Cherokee maybe as much as I did. Dad did, too. My heart kept telling me that it couldn't be true. The whole house was sad and quiet. I decided that maybe I could sleep away the sadness. I slept and I ate, nothing more. I didn't even want to sit on Mom's lap and be stroked. Mom was very concerned about me and she tried and tried to make me feel better, but nothing seemed to help. I just needed to have Cherokee back in my life, and, obviously, that just wasn't going to happen. How I missed him so!

Somewhere during this time, Mom quit her second job and was able to spend afternoons and evenings with Dad and me. It was nice, but not like having Cherokee with me. No one to cuddle with on a cold night in the comfy chair.

One day, Mom and Dad went away in the car. When they came back, they had a box with something in it. My first hope was that Cherokee had come home at last. Unfortunately, it was not Cherokee. It was a black and white male feline, but not Cherokee. They introduced us briefly, but kept him in the other room much of the time. Mom and Dad seemed to really like him, but I hated him! It took Mom a couple of days to realize it, but I knew what was wrong with him right away. Right after he tripped over me the first time. I don't even remember his name now, but there wouldn't be any point to it anyway. He got around the house pretty well, but when he bumped into the cover of the litter box, Mom realized that he was totally blind. She and Dad saw that I hated him, so back he went into the box and out the door.

It was quiet and peaceful again. I slept more and began to eat a little less. I just couldn't shake the ache in my heart.

One day, when Dad was gone for a business trip, Mom left the house for some time. When she came back, she was carrying a cardboard box with something squeaky in it. I wasn't sure I cared what was in the box, but there was a little spark of curiosity. Mom opened the box and took out what was inside.

HORRORS!!! She bought me a baby! What on earth possessed her to do such a thing? The baby was kept in the guest room and had to go see the vet almost right away because it was sneezing and coughing and had a constantly runny nose. I figured that was the last I would see of it. Boy, was I wrong! (The first time ever) Mom told me that the baby was a female and after talking to Dad on the phone, she told me the baby's name was Mina (pronounced MEE nah). However, I called her "pest." Since there was someone new in the house to keep Mom company, I began to cut my eating entirely. It was just too sad. I saw that Mina got different food from me. That was upsetting. Maybe she was getting something better. Mom tried to get me to eat a lot of different things, but I wasn't having any. One day I looked up at her and told her I was hungry (I used sign language – licking my lips with an expectant expression on my face). She looked at me and said: "I have tried giving you everything I can think of. You won't eat your dry food, you won't eat your wet food, you won't even eat tuna! What more can I do?" I almost saw the light bulb go off over her head at that moment, just like in the comics. She got the bag of Mina's food out of the closet and put some in my dish. I was feeling pretty hungry by that time, and I actually ate some of it. It really wasn't any better than my food, so I didn't finish it all, but I decided that my food was pretty good and I began eating again.

Mina became the bane of my existence for a while. I got so tired just watching her dash here and there and everywhere. Mom said we should have named her Flash. Mom tried to take pictures of Mina, but she moved so fast that mostly Mom got pictures of the floor. She was very tiny and her black and white fur made her face look round. Her tail was covered with fairly long black fur and curled up over her back. She had a lot of mischief shining from her eyes. She was afraid of me at first, but much too soon she was jumping out at me, over me, and on me. Sometimes I had to growl and hiss at her to make her settle down a little and behave. I soon took an interest in her grooming and toilet habits. In turn, Mina tried grooming me sometimes.

Mina did have one really bad habit. Mom was horrified that she would go into the litter box and bring out a little dried treasure to play with. It took a while, but she finally stopped doing that. We were Just We Two – again. Just a different two.

Well, I'm really tired after telling this part of the story. It was most exhausting. I must nap.

Yours,
Apache

More About Cherokee

Just up from my nap with the pest.

You may have noted that I usually called Cherokee stupid. There is good reason for that. Just as an example, back in Malden, whenever Mom would move her feet under the bed covers, Cherokee would jump on them. The only problem was, he forgot to be careful and would draw blood with his sharp claws and teeth, even through several layers of blankets. Mom kept telling him not to do that, but he kept on not paying any attention. Finally, she started spraying him with water every time he did it. He would stop for a couple of days and then start again. After numerous sprayings, he finally got the idea and quit - until we moved to Phoenix. He started all over again there. She started spraying again and yelling at him. He finally stopped for good. Took him long enough! Couldn't he tell that it was just her feet under the blankets and that he would hurt her with his teeth and claws? Just plain stupid!

Cherokee also had very long fur and a huge, long, furry tail, and he was also very skinny. My fur is long, but not nearly as long as his was. I found him to be the epitome of ugliness, but Mom always stood up for him and called him handsome. There's just no accounting for tastes. The pest is black and white, too, but she has a cute little round face . . . She's still just a pest! Anyway, Cherokee was not very good at taking care of himself, so I often had to wash his face for him. His long fur caused me so many hairballs I can't even begin to count them. Mom hates it when I give up hairballs; it really grosses her out. I can't help it, though. Not long after Mom adopted Cherokee, he became very matted again because of his long hair and because he didn't take care of himself.

Another of Cherokee's bad habits (as I believe I have already mentioned) was that he often would leave a very smelly deposit in the litter box. Whenever I smelled it I would rush to the box to see why there was such an odor. He usually just didn't cover them up. That really grossed me out! I would have to go into the litter box and cover it for him. Who was I - his mother? Thank goodness our litter box is covered, so the smell often did not travel too far.

"Patchy, what's a pest?"

"Go back to sleep, Pest, you don't have any place here."

"I liv hear, too. I just lern tipe."

"Go to sleep!!! You need to learn to type much better than that!"

Cherokee loved to eat! Whenever Mom would put our food down for us, he would gobble his up as fast as he could and then he would nudge me away and eat mine. What a pig! He would eat pretty much anything, so if I didn't like something, I knew that it would be eaten anyway. That sort of defeated the purpose of my not eating something, though. Sometimes I felt very sorry for him for being so skinny, and that's why I let him eat my food, too.

Whenever Mom would sit down, we would join her. I

would get comfortable on her lap and just start dropping off while she was stroking me, when, of course, Cherokee would jump up and take a place on her lap, overlapping me some. What nerve! I would put on my outraged face and jump down. He would then take over the entire lap and take up all of Mom's strokes for himself. He purred very, very loudly and it was most disturbing. Mom seemed to like it a lot, though. She would always call to me to come back, but I would just turn my back and sleep by myself. The only time Cherokee was of use to me was when it was cold and we would lie together to keep warm. Sort of reminded me of the old days on the wooded hill, with our furry family.

Well, enough for now. For some reason I can't seem to see very well just now, kind of blurry. I'm very tired. More later.

Yours,
Apache

More Ruminations

I am pretty tired today. As you can tell from previous posts, I have not been sleeping all that well. I try my best, but sometimes it just doesn't happen. Sometimes there are certain disturbances.

I have been thinking about a lot of things. I have had lots of time for that, since I've been awake so much. Take hairballs, for instance. I have them. Cherokee had them (although not nearly as many as I had, since I washed him a lot and his fur was a lot longer than mine). Pest will probably have them, too. Anyway, being a feline, I know exactly what to do with hairballs. Cough and spit them out! Mom really freaked the first time she saw one of my fine hairballs. She thought it was something I should have done in the litter box. When she realized it was composed of fur and just in the shape of my throat, she calmed down a lot.

Mom has hairballs, too. She doesn't seem to realize it, but I can tell. Every now and then she will start to cough and she will be really hacking like crazy, unable to stop. I try to signal to her what to do, but she doesn't pay any attention. I look at her and then I look at the floor. I do it several times, but she manages to stop coughing without giving up the hairball. She's probably doing some sort of internal damage to herself, but it's her decision. You can't blame me; I try.

I also have thought a lot about rain. What is the point? It just gets everything wet and makes the air wet, too.

Sometimes the rain makes a lot of crashing noises and flashes bright lights. That's a little scary. It's always nice to cuddle up to Mom when that happens, or go under the bed, but Mom is best. At least we haven't had much rain since we moved to Phoenix. I could get to like it here a lot.

Another thing to think about is company. Why do we have to have any? We are just fine without them. They smell different, sometimes they smell very bad. They talk to Mom a lot and she doesn't have time for us when they are here. They also make a loud noise with the doorbell. It hurts my ears, and I always run upstairs and go under the bed. I don't like strangers in the house.

The only company (stranger) that I liked was Mom's grandson, whose name is Richie. He came to stay for a while during a couple of summers. He liked us and we liked him. He was fun sometimes and would play with Cherokee. I liked to watch. Every now and then he would feed us or give us treats, too. There are some good treats out there! Treats are probably better than geckos. I wouldn't mind if he came back. I also liked it when Mom's daughter, Linda, visited. She wasn't here nearly as much as Mom's grandson, though.

I like it when Mom brings flowers into the house. Some of them taste very good, but Mom gets upset when the vase tips over and water gets on the table. I think my favorite flowers are what Mom calls baby's breath. They are just yummy, but it's a little hard to get them out of the vase without pulling out the rest of the flowers and tipping over the vase. Life is just imperfect sometimes.

Food! Where does it come from, anyway? Mom says

she is going shopping, or going to the store. When she comes back, she has food in bags. Some of it she puts in the refrigerator, like meat, wonderful meat. The rest goes into various cupboards. But what is this "store?" Does she go to this "store" and they just hand her bags of stuff? Would they give me bags of meat? Would I even be able to find a "store?"

Toilet water! Why am I not allowed to drink it? It is cool and tasty. Mom says I get sick after drinking it. I doubt it. Cherokee liked it, too. He always made a big mess with water all over the place. Mom tries to be sure that the toilet lid is closed at all times. Killjoy!

Well, I shall leave you with those thoughts. I feel a nap coming on and must take advantage of it when it happens. I need my beauty sleep!

Yours,
Apache

Happy Home

M-m-m-m! A nice rest! It's so good to sleep.

"Patchy, Patchy!"

"That's Miss Apache to you. What do you want, Pest? Besides, I'm busy. Go away!"

As I said, the Pest can call me Miss, as I have never been married. Judging by Cherokee, I'm glad I never was. He annoyed me no end sometimes, just like Pest. Mom used to share my view of marriage, saying that she would never get married again. Sometimes men would come over and take her away for a while, but they never moved in. Things have changed considerably, but I will get to that later.

"Miss Patchy! Miss Patchy!"

"What now?"

"Where Mr. Cherokee? I like meet him."

"Well, you can't. Go to sleep, or go play with your tail or something!"

"I think I like Mr. Cherokee. He like play. When he come home?"

"He won't ever come home again, so forget about him.

Now, go away."

"Miss Patchy, why you eyes wet? You cry? Why you cry?"

"Just go away and leave me alone. What a pest!"

"I no pest, I think, but I go 'way. We play later."

"Don't bet on it!"

What a way to have a good mood spoiled! There are few enough of them as it is.

Anyway, where was I? Oh yes, the three of us were settled into our Phoenix home. Mom was home most of the time for a while and Cherokee and I really enjoyed that. We did a lot of cuddling, and she made sure we were fed at the right times and that the litter box was kept clean. She always told us that she loved us and that made us feel so special, because we loved her, too. That's why neither Cherokee nor I would ever have bitten or scratched her. Not for anything! Except totally by accident during rough play. This is one area where Cherokee became a bit of a hero.

After we got settled in after our big move to Phoenix, Mom took each of us to see the vet. I sure hated it when I went, but I behaved pretty well. When it was Cherokee's time to see the vet, he was really upset. Mom had to chase him all over the house in order to get him into the box. We had what Mom said was a loft room overlooking the couch room. The TV holder was up against the wall in the couch room, just under the open area from upstairs. I think it was twice that Cherokee ran upstairs, jumped up on the half-wall and down onto the entertainment center. From there, he jumped all the way down to the floor. It's surprising that he didn't break a leg or anything. Well, Mom finally got the idea to close all the doors and Cherokee took refuge in the downstairs bathroom. He kept making the same mistake over and over again, didn't he.

She finally got him into the box and took him out to the car and off they went. Mom tells people what Cherokee did there. He was very unhappy and frightened, and put up quite a fight when they took him into the back room. The vet came out bleeding and said that Cherokee had bitten him. Hooray!!! My hero! Mom had to fax a copy of his rabies vaccination certificate from Malden so that the doctor would be a little happier. I think that's the last time Mom took Cherokee to the vet until much later on.

Mom took me to the vet a second time, and they needed, of all things, some of my urine. Ugh! What on earth did they want that for? Didn't they have any of their own? Needless to say, Mom could not get any from me (she could never be sure what was mine and what was Cherokee's), so they had to take it from me in the back room. One of us was fighting mad and moving around a lot, so some of it got on my fur. Very disgusting! I didn't even want to lick myself clean. They offered to clean me, but Mom said that she would do it at home. She should have let them, maybe I could have gotten in a few bites and scratches.

When we got home, Mom didn't let me out of the box right away, but took me upstairs to her bathroom. She put my box in the shower stall, with me in it, took off her clothes and got into the shower stall, too. She turned on the warm water and opened the box. There was no way I was leaving that box, at least not on my own power. Mom upended the box and I was forced to get out. I got thoroughly wet and was very angry. Mom just would not let me back into the box. She had a towel on the shower door, and after turning off the water, she wrapped me in the towel and held it on me for a little while. I didn't like that either, though, so I struggled out of the towel and went somewhere to dry myself off. At least the urine was off me! If I never see another vet, it will be too soon. Of course, I have been a few times since then, but I hope never to go again. It is always unpleasant, to say the least.

One time, not too long ago, Mom took me to a different vet. Again, they took me, struggling, into the back room. I don't struggle when Mom holds me, but they won't let that happen. They say it is too dangerous. For whom? Not for Mom. Anyway, I was struggling and screaming for help. They did some awful things to me and then brought me back, screaming, hissing and spitting. Also scratching. They were filled with fear and quickly put me down on the floor of the room with Mom and the box and warned Mom that I might hurt her. She just laughed and came over to where I was sheltering under the counter, picked me up and stroked me a little and I let her put me in the box. She knew I wouldn't hurt her and I knew she wouldn't hurt me.

Well, all these memories are making me tired. Maybe I'll see if Mom is eating anything good for lunch that she might share with me, and then I'll take a well-deserved nap. Ya-a-a-wn!

Yours,
Apache

Oops!

"Well, now is my chance to show what I have learned. I think this is a lot of fu . . .!"

"What are you doing??"

"Oh, Miss Patchy, I thought you were asleep."

"Well, I was, but you are making a lot of noise!"

"I'm sorry (not), but I wanted to show you what I can do."

"JUST! STEP! AWAY! FROM! THE KEYBOARD!"

"Okay, Miss Patchy, but my time will come."

"Just go to sleep."

"But I'm not sleepy."

"Just go! Go play with Mousey or something. Chase your tail; you're good at that!"

"Ha! Someday, Miss Patchy, someday."

What nerve! There I was, sleeping peacefully here in the office, when Pest started making all that noise. Clicking on the keys, giggling! No matter, she's gone now and I can get down to business.

You know, people often wonder why I am called Apache and why my brother was called Cherokee. I don't think anyone really knows. Maybe they ran out of names at the foster home. Mom thinks it was an omen or something. She said that, when she adopted us back there in Malden, she had no idea that she would ever move to Phoenix. She said it never had entered her mind. However, since we had had those names for a few years, she didn't feel it would be right to change them. And she was right, of course. Mom usually is right. Not right as often as I am, since I am never wrong, but usually right.

Names can be handy things. I was surprised to learn some years ago that humans have names. They all look so much alike (with color differences) that I always just sort of lumped them all together and called them humans. I guess it helps that they have names, because it makes it easier to tell them apart. If I say to someone that there's a human at the door, it doesn't mean a whole lot. They are a dime a dozen, so to speak. But if I say that Bob is at the door, then we know right away just who is at the door - friend, enemy, or stranger. We will run up under the bed anyway, but it's nice to know just who you are avoiding.

I think I mentioned toilets before. They seem like rather strange things, but I guess humans have slightly different needs. None of them would ever fit into our litter box, so the bathroom, with its toilet, is good for them. Cherokee was always totally fascinated by the toilet. He would drink out of it, too, but his interest went much further. He couldn't get enough of watching it flush. He told me that he loved to watch it swirl around and disappear. Then suddenly, it would come back again, but without any stuff in it. He tried so hard to understand what was happening and how it worked. At one time, Mom actually tried to get us to use the toilet instead of the litter box. What a hoot! At first, there was this plastic hanging from the seat and there was a little bit of litter in it. That was okay, and we did use it. Then, one day Mom removed the plastic and the litter and that wasn't okay. I didn't like hanging over that water and neither did Cherokee. We left her a message in the bathroom sink that we didn't like it and she never tried it again. Hooray for the litter box!

Now the bathtub is something else. It would appear to be something totally useless, but Mom persists in filling it with water every now and then and sitting in it. Ugh! I just don't understand that mindset. It did cause us some amusement, though. Mom would always remove her fur, or I mean her clothes, before she would get into all that hot water. How funny! Kind of a little embarrassing, too. Cherokee and I would really get a kick out of seeing her that way. Humans are so funny looking. Laughter is really very good for people of all kinds. Being incredibly curious, Cherokee tried to figure out what she was doing in the tub and managed to fall in once. ONCE! He didn't try that again, unlike some other people I know.

Did I ever mention human food? Some of it is really great, like beef, chicken, turkey, lamb, even pork. I don't understand why Mom eats all that other stuff, though. Eggs I can see, even cheese sometimes, but corn? Celery? Tomatoes? Bananas? Oranges? Yech!!!! I gag just thinking about those things. About the only other thing I like is a little bit of ice cream. Mom says that sugar is not good for us, so it's only just once in a great while that she gives me a tiny taste of ice cream. I like mint, vanilla, and strawberry ice cream. She says that all the felines she has ever had liked strawberry ice cream. Oh, I forgot about fish! That is delicious, too. Even in a can, like tuna. It's really great when she cooks salmon and gives me a few bites. Yum!!

Mom does give us good, wet food from a can most of the time, along with that dry stuff. I can see why Cherokee started putting some of his in the water dish, because I find that I am now beginning to like it that way myself. It seems to be a lot harder these days. Have they changed the recipe? Once in a while, she runs out of canned food and has to use canned tuna. It's not supposed to be very good for us, but Mom says that a rare treat is okay.

Well, I think we are going to watch a movie or TV or something now. It's too bad we don't have a lot of cable channels anymore. Cherokee and I used to love watching Animal Planet with Mom. Sometimes Cherokee would get so excited that he would accidently change the channel by stepping on the remote control. Silly goof! We weren't terribly interested in watching the dog stuff, but there were a lot of felines on TV, too.

I will probably end up sleeping through most of the movie or whatever. I do have some sleeping to catch up on, since Pest disturbed me. Wish me a good nap!

Yours,
Apache

My Name is Mina

It's a little bit boring right now. I've been trying to play with Miss Patchy, but she got angry and growled and hissed at me and went back to sleep. All she does is sleep. I don't think she feels very good. I've heard Mom and Dad talking about Miss Patchy going to the vet on Monday to have dental surgery. They are a little worried, but they want her to feel better and maybe have some more energy. I think that would be great! I would like it if she would play with me.

When I first met Mom, I was curled up in a cage with two of my sisters. We were sleeping at the time, but we were always ready to play. They took the three of us into a little room where Mom was sitting. My sisters went all over the place, but I kind of liked Mom and decided to climb up into her lap. It was a very nice lap, and I thought maybe she would be staying with us. That was not to be the case, though. They put me back with my sisters, but not for long. They then put me in a cardboard box with a few small holes in it and a handle. It was locked so I couldn't get out. I was pretty scared, but Mom tried to comfort me. I cried a lot, but she kept scratching on the outside of the box and I was quiet while I tried to figure out what was making the noise. When Mom and I left the place where I had been in a cage with my sisters, she walked for quite a little way and then we sat for a while. I heard a lot of noise outside the box, and it was scary.

Finally, a big noisy thing came along and stopped by us, hissing as it did so. Mom and I got into it and we rolled away. That was scary, too. Lots of strange people and smells. After a little while, we got off – Mom said it was called a bus – and did some more walking. Not too much later, we went inside a place. It smelled good, like other felines. It was still scary, though, because it did not smell like my sisters or my furry mom. Anyway, Mom gently took me out of the box and showed me to Miss Patchy. She introduced us, but Miss Patchy growled and hissed and did not seem to be happy to meet me. Mom said that I had to live in a separate room for a little while, so that Miss Patchy and I could get used to being in the same house. I found a place to hide, under the sofa bed. I was very small. Mom was upset and finally managed to get me out. She stuffed towels around the bottom of the sofa bed so I couldn't get under there. I learned to move the towels from around the sofa bed not long after I moved in, but now I'm too big to fit under there.

In my room there was a furry bed with a little blanket, a litter pan and food and water dishes. All the comforts of home, except for my sisters. I missed them very much. My room had a cement floor and it was cold. Some of it was covered with a rug, and Mom brought in what she called a radiator to keep the room warm for me. Nonetheless, I began to cough and sneeze and my nose was running all the time. After a couple of days, Mom put me back in the box. I thought maybe I was going back to live with my sisters, but, instead, we walked to the vet. They did some nasty things to me and then we walked back home. Mom had some medicine that she had to give me, and she put stuff in our food, too. She also got a little thing (she called it a humidifier) that made the air a little wet. It made it a little easier for me to breathe.

When I got better, Mom let me go out into the house for a while every day, so Miss Patchy and I could get acquainted. She still was not very friendly to me, but she didn't hurt me – she just stayed away from me.

It wasn't long before I was able to go upstairs and I discovered THE BED! It was soft and warm when Mom and Dad were in it. I used to go under the covers and sleep between the two of them. Miss Patchy stayed out on top of the covers. Mom was always afraid that either she or Dad would roll over on me, but I was pretty quick to move if they did. It was in the bed that I learned a new sentence. "Lie down and go to sleep." The first time Mom said it, I knew exactly what she wanted me to do, and I did it. She was very surprised that I knew it right away. She always tells me how smart I am, so why should she be surprised?

My new home came with lots of toys. Later, Miss Patchy told me that all the toys had belonged to her and Mr. Cherokee, but only Mr. Cherokee liked to play. He was no longer there, so the toys were now mine. There were lots of fun things, and I was constantly busy playing with them, except when I fell asleep, which was a lot. I kept dashing from one toy to another, trying to play with all of them, so none of them would feel left out. There was a ring with a ball inside, a stick with a string on it, and lots of little mice. There were other things, too, but those are my favorites.

Dad wasn't home when I moved in, but he joined us a little later. I could tell that he liked me a lot, and he has since proved that to me. I love to help him on the computer and sit on his lap, or lie up on top of the computer desk. It is kind of high, so I can see everything from there. With Mom, I like to hug. I get up on her lap, reach up and put my arms around her neck. I then knead her neck and purr a lot. She loves it, but keeps telling me to be careful with my claws, because it hurts her. She never tells me to get down, though, so I think she likes it as much as I do.

Miss Patchy has taught me that I should sleep all day, like her, so I do that most of the time. I am then ready to play at night. When Mom and Dad get into bed and turn out the lights, I get up on the dresser and play with the chain that is hanging down the wall. It makes a really nice noise when it hits the wall. Unfortunately, Mom and Dad don't appreciate it the way I do and make me leave the bedroom and then shut the door on me. Maybe someday I will be like Miss Patchy and sleep all day and all night. Sounds boring, though!

The temperatures seem much warmer these days, than when I moved in. Mom says it is summer now and it is very hot outside. Something fascinating is going on now in the house. Sometimes when we are in a room, I will feel a little breeze coming from above. When I look up, I see something turning around on the ceiling. I want so much to get up there to investigate, but so far have not discovered a way to do that. I have investigated most of the house, but a few things remain to be done. Hopefully, I will be able to do them before long.

Well, Miss Patchy is telling me that it is time to sleep some more, so I will go now, but I would rather play.

Regards,
Mina

More From Mina

Well, I'm feeling pretty good today. Of course, I always do, so that's not news, I guess. I was a little lonely on Monday, though. That morning, they put Miss Patchy in the box and took her away. I tried and tried to get her out of the box before they left, but I couldn't find the way to open the door. I was a little scared. She was scared, too. What if she didn't come back? They said she would be back in the afternoon. I was sure hoping that it was true! Fortunately, she did come back later on when the sun was starting to go down. All she wanted to do was sleep, though, and she growled at me a little when I wanted to play with her. She didn't eat anything for supper, and then Mom squirted something into her mouth and she went to sleep again. I think her mouth was hurting her.

I didn't think I would miss Miss Patchy, because she is so old and boring, but sometimes she licks my face and grooms my fur. She talks to me and explains things to me – almost like a mother. I would have been very sorry if she hadn't come back. We are getting to be very good friends. I hardly ever miss my sisters or furry mother these days. Sometimes I can't even remember what they look like. It's almost as though I have always lived here with Miss Patchy and Mom and Dad.

I'm pretty much all grown up now, but I still love to play. Miss Patchy says she gets tired just watching me run around, but I need exercise. It wouldn't hurt Miss Patchy to exercise, either. Mom says that she has gained a lot of weight, and Dad calls her "Fatty Girl" sometimes. Mom has been giving us less food, but all Miss Patchy does is sleep and eat (she eats most of my food, too), so she just gets fat.

On Tuesday morning, Miss Patchy was still pretty sleepy and cranky. She ate something, so I think she was feeling better. After eating, though, her mouth started to hurt again, so Mom and Dad held her down while she screamed and growled and hissed and Mom squirted that stuff in her mouth again. Mom said that it stressed everyone so much (especially Miss Patchy) that she wasn't going to squirt the stuff in Miss Patchy's mouth any more. That was okay, since Miss Patchy seemed to feel a lot better later on that day.

Yesterday, when Mom got up in the morning and went downstairs to feed us, Miss Patchy was running down the steps right beside me. She kept up with me! She has always very slowly walked down the steps since I have known her. Maybe she won't be so mad when I leap over her now. Maybe she will play with me!

Miss Patchy says that the vet took some of her teeth away. They were hurting her anyway, so she doesn't miss them very much. The vet must have given her some energy, too, because she is much more awake now. I can hardly wait to play with her. We can have lots of fun.

I have to go play now, so please excuse me.

Regards,
Mina

The Dreaded Vet

Well, I just had a little nap. I find that I really don't need to sleep as much as I used to, but I still enjoy my naps very much. I see that Pest has been filling in for me on this blog. I was grateful to her for trying to get me out of the box, but let me explain all that happened to me during the time that I was not writing.

On Monday, Mom and Dad managed to get me into the infamous box. Mom picked me up out of the bathtub where I was enjoying a little privacy. I spread out my back legs so that she couldn't get me into the box (which was standing on its end), but Dad helped her out by holding my back legs together so Mom could put me in. Oh, I was so angry! I hate going into that box. It is a death box, although in this case that was not true.

After being so unceremoniously dumped into the box, we went out to the car and rolled away. We went to the vet's place, but a different one than we went to last time. I think I had seen this vet before, maybe last year or sometime. That didn't make me like it any better, though. I hissed and growled at the vet (well, actually her assistant) to demonstrate my anger and displeasure at being treated so badly. They really treated me well; I was just very unhappy to be in that box and being anywhere but home. My teeth were hurting and I was in no mood for that sort of thing.

I was there for quite a while before they tried to take

me out of the box. I just would not let them. I got myself as far back in the box as I could and braced myself totally with all four legs. I growled and hissed. The vet said she was going to call Mom. When she came back, they put my box into a big clear plastic box and then I fell asleep. When I woke up, my mouth hurt a lot, even more than before, and I felt something strange in it, where one of my precious teeth used to be. They had taken some of my teeth! Did they want them for something, some sort of ritual? I just couldn't understand. I was so sleepy that I didn't really have time to think about it. I guess I sort of dozed off and on for a while, and then I heard Mom's voice calling me. Oh, blessed day! I was so happy to hear her voice that I calmly let them pick up the box and take it out to the other room. There, waiting for me, were Mom and Dad. Happiness!! Dad carried me out to the car and off we rolled, until I could smell home.

Seeing the inside of my home made me feel much better, but my mouth still hurt quite a bit. I let Mom take me out of the box, but I just wanted to lie down and sleep. When she called us for supper, I went into the food room, wobbly as I was, but I didn't seem to be hungry. Not long after that, Mom squirted something in my mouth and I soon went to sleep on my heart-shaped cushion on the floor.

The next morning, I ate my breakfast, since I was very hungry. I even crunched some of Mina's dry food. That might have been a mistake, because my mouth hurt a lot after that. Mom and Dad then held me down and she squirted some more of that stuff in my mouth. I struggled and screamed, to no avail. She finally managed to get it into my mouth. Mom said that it was so stressful for everyone squirting that stuff into my mouth that she was not going to do it again. Thank goodness! I slept again after that, but when I woke up later, I felt pretty good. My mouth was feeling much better, and I felt much more awake than before. Mina wanted to play, but I still didn't feel too much like playing.

On Wednesday morning, I felt so good that I actually ran down the stairs, keeping up completely with Mina. I felt as though I had some energy. Maybe later I will play a little, even though I have never been much for playing. That was always Cherokee's job. I wish he were here. He always wanted to wrestle, and now I feel as though I could do that. Maybe one day Mina and I will wrestle. She is becoming a nice companion. She listens to me when I tell her things; she is eager to learn from me. It's almost as if she considered me to be her mother.

On that note, I think I will go take a nap so that I can contemplate the happenings of this strange week.

Yours,
Apache

Thoughts

Pain free at last! Did the vet do that? It doesn't seem right that such an unpleasant experience should take away my tooth pain.

I don't seem to sleep as much as before. Is that good or is it bad? I don't know. I have just had a good nap, though, and I was in the office with Mom. For the first time in quite a while, I actually felt like getting up in the chair with her. I think the chair got a little smaller, or Mom got a little bigger, but it was pretty tight. I stayed for a while, and Mom thanked me for coming up, saying that it had been quite a while.

Mom calls me her "pretty girl." I like that. She calls me "Beauty" and she calls Mina "Cutie." Mina really kisses up by getting up on Mom's lap, putting her front legs around Mom's neck, kneading, purring, and burrowing her little head in under Mom's chin. Mom just eats it up! It's pretty disgusting, if you ask me. Cherokee used to kiss up, too. I would get up in that comfy chair with Mom and, after a few minutes, Cherokee would come galloping in and jump up in the chair. I always left after that and went to lie on the couch by myself. It didn't seem to matter to Cherokee that I was glaring at him. He just kept on purring and putting his head under Mom's hand so she would pet him. Completely disgusting! Mina does that little head under the hand thing, also.

Mom really tries to be fair to everyone,

though. Whenever she leaves the house, she always says goodbye to everyone. Now, it's Dad first, then me, then Mina. I used to be first, before Dad came. Oh well, I'm glad Dad's here anyway. When Mom comes home from wherever it is she has been, she says: "Babies, I'm home!" It's always nice to be recognized and appreciated. She really likes it when we come downstairs to greet her.

When we get Mom up in the morning (when it starts getting light), she tells us "good morning," and asks us if we would like some breakfast. Kind of a silly question, if you ask me! Of course we want breakfast! We're pretty hungry after a whole night without food. At night, she'll call out "Supper!" and we always come into the food room or down the stairs to eat. A number of years ago, Cherokee and I got only wet food. Then someone told Mom that wet food wasn't really good for us and she started feeding us dry food only. It was okay, but not nearly as good as wet food. Now she makes food for us and we get a combination of wet food out of the can, some of her homemade food, and dry food. It's pretty satisfactory. We often leave a little dry food for later on, in case we get hungry again.

The first food she made was not that great. It had a kind of funny taste in it. She said she had cooked chicken thighs and catfish nuggets. She ground them up and then added egg and Vitamin E. Something just didn't taste quite right. A couple of days ago, she made a second batch of food – chicken thighs and beef heart, with soft-boiled egg. Yummy! She gave Mina and me a few little slices of raw beef heart. It was so wonderful! Even Mina loved it, and she never seemed to care for raw meat. She can give me beef heart anytime, raw or cooked! I wonder what the next batch will be like.

Well, thinking of eating is making me sleepy. I need to take a nap until the next meal.

Yours,
Apache

Where Do Humans Come From?

Good morning! I've been awake for a while now and have eaten a delicious breakfast – all of it. I was so hungry that I actually ran down the stairs again. Haven't done that for a while.

I've been pondering some things. Where DO humans come from? As I said before, I have never actually seen a baby human, so I have no idea what they look like. I had always assumed that they might look like adult humans, just not so big – like felines. I'm beginning to question that assumption. Dad says he is from a Turkey. ???? I think turkeys are birds, at least that's what Mom calls the one we eat on Thanksgiving. What do humans and birds have to do with each other? This is very puzzling. Mom says that she is from Ohio. What is an Ohio? Is it also a bird? I certainly have never seen an Ohio. I always say that I am from Malden, but what is a Malden? I had always thought that that is what we called the house we lived in there, but I'm beginning to wonder now. I vaguely remember my feline mom, and she looked just like any feline, just bigger than her kittens. Mina says that she remembers her feline mom, too. What is it about humans?

Mom talks about others who are also from Ohio, but some from Indiana, Chicago, Boston, California, etc. Are these all birds? Or what? Certainly Dad does not look like a turkey, as much as I can tell. He definitely is not a bird, as he doesn't have wings or skinny feet, or feathers. But none of the turkeys I have seen have skinny feet (or any feet), and they don't have feathers. Sometimes Mom pulls a part off the turkey and calls it a wing. She says they are delicious. Hm-m-m-m! What is going on here? Our house is called Phoenix, but I have heard Mom say that there are three and a half million people in Phoenix. Where are they all? They certainly aren't here in our house, unless I am misunderstanding numbers. Maybe someday Mom will explain things to me. I have a feeling that there are a lot of things in the human area that I don't understand at all.

Here are some other things about humans that I just don't get. Why do they persist in eating fruits and vegetables and chocolate? Don't they know that those things are not good for them? I would never, ever eat them; they taste awful!

Why do they do what they call "going to work?" Where is work and what do they do there? They call it "having a job." All I know is that they are gone from the house for a while and then they come home. Do they go somewhere and just sit around? Do they watch TV there? Are there felines there? When Mom had two jobs, she said that she was completely exhausted and felt that she was dying. She would get up in the morning, feed us, clean our litter box, eat something yucky and then drive away. She would come home late at night when it had been dark for a while, long after our hunger had begun and she would feed us. Then she would sit in the comfy chair and turn on the TV for a little while before she would go to bed. She said that she was "wired" and couldn't sleep right away after she came home. Cherokee and I would get up in the chair with her so that she could pet us and make us feel good. It wasn't much fun for us when she worked two jobs; we missed her a lot. When Dad came, it was better because we had company all day and then Mom would come home at night. When she started going to work for just a little while, it was much better for us. We had lots of company then. We had our choice of Dad or Mom. That's how it is now, and Mina and I are happy with it.

All of this brain work, this contemplation of things that cannot be understood, is exhausting me. I must take a long nap now. Perhaps I will dream the answers to all of my questions.

Yours,
Apache

Mina's Thoughts

Whee!!!! What fun it is to be alive and play! I just played with the ball in the ring and it makes such a great noise. I'm taking just a short break so I can write. It isn't often that I have time or that the computer is free, so I must take advantage of it when it comes up.

First of all, I want to say that playing is my life! There are so many great things to play with. Besides the ball in the ring, squeaky mousies and other things, I now have a wonderful ball that Dad brought back for me from away. I don't know where away is, but there must be a lot of nice toys there. Maybe Dad will take me to away some day so I can see all the toys. Other things I love to play with are some little paper packages that smell nice. Mom has them on the tray on the table with the salt and pepper. She gets mad when I take them and tells me not to play with the mints. I do anyway. There also is the little brush up on the bathroom counter that smells like Mom's mouth. It is just tiny and plastic. She gets mad about that, too. Lately, I have been trying for the cold things in the glass Mom drinks from. Once I get one out of the glass, I play with it for a while (as long as I can stand the cold of it), but then I must forget where I put it, because it is never there when I come back.

Another fun toy is the big chain that hangs down the wall of the bedroom. It makes a wonderful loud noise when I pull on it, let it go, and it bangs against the wall. For some reason, Mom or Dad will always get up out of bed and shut me out of the room when I do that. They also don't seem to like it when I mine for their fingers under the pillows. One toy that Mom really hates is what she calls the "nuggets" that I get out of the litter box. They are fun. They are very hard and they make a nice noise when I drop them on the tile floor. Mom can always tell when I have one and she will yell at me and take it away. Mom and Dad just don't know how to play at all.

I had an experience a little while ago. It was pretty scary. Mom went out on the roof and, of course, I dashed out after her. Something was wrong with it that time, though. It was dark, and the air around me was moving a lot and there were flashes of light in the sky. The air just made my hair stand up and it was very, very scary. I panicked, I guess, and I ran to the door, but it was closed, so I ran and jumped up on the wall that divides the parts of the roof. Mom grabbed me off the wall and took me, struggling, to the door. Before she could open it, I gave one last strong struggle and I scratched her on the leg. She didn't even yell at me, but made sure I was in the house. She knew that I was afraid, so she didn't do or say anything to me. I'm really sorry that I scratched her, but I was just so scared. Mom put alcohol on the scratch and then tried to comfort me. I love Mom a lot!

There was another scary time, but it was a long time ago. Mom and Dad went to away and they were gone all day. Mom got something out of the closet before they left, and I, naturally, dashed into the closet so they couldn't see me. Then they closed the door and left. There I was, all alone in the dark. I went to the door and called out, but no one was home except Miss Patchy, and she doesn't know how to open doors. I was very frightened and lonely, but at least I could talk to Miss Patchy. I didn't have a litter box in there, so I had to leave something on the carpet. When Mom and Dad got home, I was frantic, and I was screaming and crying at the door. Mom looked in my room and when she didn't find me there, she checked the closet. I was so happy to get out. Mom and Dad were upset that they had shut me in the closet and now they always check before they shut doors. Of course, I do my part by always letting them know that I am in there. As I dash in (while they are watching), I call out to let them know. I don't ever want to be shut in there again. I've also been shut in the garage a couple of times. I don't like that, either, so I always let them know I'm going out there so they don't forget me.

Another experience that took place a while ago, was that I got outside. They will never know how, and I'm not going to tell them, because I might want to go out again. It was pretty cold out there, and very dark, and I heard strange things moving. I was outside until it started to get light. When I didn't come to breakfast, Mom started calling me and looking for me. I was very small and didn't have a big voice, but Mom finally opened the front door, and she saw my cold, little body and quickly brought me inside. I ate my breakfast and we cuddled a little and I finally got warm. I don't like it much outside, even though it's not cold out there now, but maybe it's cold only when it's dark. Sometimes, Mom will let us go out on the patio when she is out there, and it's very hot out there now. It used to be cold. Is it me, or is something changing in the air?

Well, I see a toy that needs to be played with, so I must dash off now.

Regards,
Mina

Mina Has a Lot to Learn

Well, I've had a nice nap and I'm ready to rumble, as I've heard humans say. I've heard it on the TV. I'm not sure exactly what it means, but it sounds good.

Speaking of rumbling, Mina was out on the roof a while ago, and she got very scared, as I think she wrote in her last post. Of course, it was thunder and lightning and wind that she experienced. She was extremely frightened. Ha! Ha! She is so curious and nosy, it serves her right. However, she keeps on being curious and nosy, no matter what happens. She usually learns from her experiences, so all is not lost, but she makes me laugh a lot.

Lately, I have been feeling pretty good. What a nice change from before! Mom has noticed it, too, and claims that I have lost weight, as well. That's really good news. She says that my face is thinner and I'm looking very good. Mina just thinks I look old, no matter what. Just wait until she is my age! She has been jumping at me a lot lately, and starting fights. We wrestle a lot, but I always win, since she is very small and I am not so small. Sometimes she keeps it up long after I'm tired of it. That's when I get mad and growl and hiss at her. It takes her a little while, but she usually realizes that it's time to quit.

When I lie down for a nap, Mina usually comes with me, but Mom has noticed that quite often Mina is lying there with her eyes open, looking bored. Silly girl! She just doesn't know what is good for her. One can never get enough sleep. Or enough good food, although I haven't been eating as much as before. I think Mom is giving us a little less food, and I just don't seem to be that hungry these days. Maybe the food Mom makes for us is a little more satisfying. The first time she made food for us, we didn't like it an awful lot, as I mentioned previously, but this second batch is very good. Mom always gives me a little bit of yogurt with my meal. At first, I didn't like it at all, and Mina won't touch it, but I do eat it now, although I usually leave it for last.

Mom has made up some new names for us. She calls me Queen Patchy and she calls Mina Princess Mina. She uses those names only sometimes, but I rather like mine. It makes me feel very regal, I think is the word I want. Mina doesn't care one way or the other. Pretty much all she's interested in is her toys. I keep reminding her that they are actually Cherokee's toys (most of them, anyway), but she doesn't care. She thinks she would have liked to know Cherokee, but, of course, that will never happen. I still miss him so much, but I am not as sad as I was before. I guess that's good, but I don't ever want to forget my precious brother. Perhaps when my time comes, Mina will miss me.

Mom and Dad are now talking about moving somewhere. They say that the economy is so bad that they just don't know what they will do. Dad has not been able to find a job – any job, and Mom is really worried about money. I never worry about money. I'm not even sure what it is for, but Mom and Dad say they never have enough of it. As long as I have a home and food, I'm not worried about anything.

I wish this "bad economy" would go away, since it is making Mom and Dad unhappy and worried. I don't know what it is, so I don't know what it looks like, but if I ever find out and see it somewhere, I will growl and hiss at it, bite it and scratch it and make it go away. Then we can all be happy once more. One can never overrate happiness. It is a wonderful way of life. I can never get enough of it. Food makes me happy, Mom and Dad make me happy, naps make me happy. What more could there be to life?

Mom says she has meat in the freezer that she will cook for us soon, since the second batch of food is getting low. That makes me happy, because I know that we will be eating well for a long time.

Well, all this worry on Mom and Dad's part is making me very tired. I think maybe a nap would do wonders for this problem. Maybe Mom and Dad should do more of it. That's it for now.

Yours,
Apache

Mina's Rebuttal

What fun! I've been lying on the table in the office, on the papers and things that are there. Before that, I was in a box on the table. The table is a really fun place, so many little things to scatter. There are lots of other things to do today, but I will get to them later. Just the other day, I scattered the bits of paper by the shredder. That is a lot of fun, too.

There are so many amusing things to do in the office. When I get a little tired, I jump up on the top of the computer desk. That means that I jump on the desk, then up on top of the monitor, and then up to the top, over the shelves and things. There are four pictures hanging on the wall over the computer desk. Mom says they are pictures of her, her two sisters, and her brother. I like to play with her brother's picture, which is hanging just over where I like to lie down. Mom used to straighten it up every time I made it crooked, but now she just leaves it the way it is. She's just no fun at all. It was a great game.

Just the other day, we were all on the couch, watching a movie. I was up on the top of the back cushions and Mom was lying down next to Dad. I got tired of the movie, so I jumped down hard on her stomach. I don't know why, but she didn't find that as much fun as I did. Yesterday we watched another movie. Mom said it was called "Lady and the Tramp." I watched a lot of it, because there were lots of dogs in it and sometimes they barked. It's kind of silly to make a movie about dogs, since felines are much more interesting. I guess everyone likes different things in life. Mom says that a lot of people have dogs, and I do hear them barking sometimes. Felines are *so much quieter and, I think, better behaved, although I really haven't known any dogs.*

I haven't gone out on the roof since my scary experience. I'm not sure I will go out there ever again. Mom keeps telling me now that it's very hot out there and I wouldn't like it anyway. It's hot in the garage, too, so I never like to stay out there for very long. The patio is pretty hot, too, but there is shade, and sometimes the air moves a little bit. We go out there only in the morning. Mom says that is before it gets really hot outside. We've been out there a few times lately, because Mom thinks maybe her purple lilac vine has died. I'm not sure what that is, but she is sad about it. She has given it water a few times, and even what she calls food, but she thinks it is gone. That makes her sad, so I am sad, too. Poor purple lilac vine!

Miss Patchy thinks it's odd that I lie down with her for a nap, but keep my eyes open. Who wouldn't? It is boring! Somehow she can just lie there sleeping, for hours and hours. A lot of the time, she sleeps under Mom and Dad's bed. Another boring place! Sometimes I like to sleep in the water box. Mom and Dad buy bottles of water and keep the packages on the floor in the eating room. When some of the bottles have been taken out, I like to crawl in there. I chew on the plastic covering for a while and then sometimes I sleep. The water packages are kept right under the window, which is another fun thing to do. I like to get up on the window sill and look out. Sometimes those buzz birds come near and tease me. Ooooh! Would I love to get my paws on one of those!

The other day, Mom was going out on the patio, and I rushed to go out as soon as she opened the door. I bounced right back! I could feel the hot air coming in, and the sounds of the outside were coming in, and I could see out, but I couldn't get through. Mom laughed and said I had to wait until she opened the screen. Oh! Not sure what it is exactly, but now I know to watch for it. I didn't realize it was there, since I could see through it. If I look closely, though, I can see it. Sometimes humans have funny things. I will have to learn more about these screens. It was kind of an embarrassing moment.

Well, I think I see some things that need to be played with, so I will end for now, but I will be back.

Regards,
Mina

Things

I just finished playing with a great toy! I'm not sure how to describe it, but it curves up on one side and down on the other. It has interesting things on it, too. It was lots of fun reaching under it and playing with the little ball that is attached to it. I can move it around on the floor, too, and that makes a nice noise. Mom heard it and came to see what I was doing. She didn't yell at me or call me "bad girl," so it must be okay to play with it. Maybe I'll leave it alone for a while.

I've been noticing some things about Mom and Dad, well mostly Mom. Sometimes I see her without her clothes on, and she is really funny-looking. I was very surprised to see that she has only two milk holders. My feline mom had lots of them. Of course, just seeing the milk holders made me realize that probably human babies get their milk that way, just the way we felines do. I know that Miss Patchy has wondered sometimes about baby humans and whether they actually exist, since she has never seen one, but now I think I know that they do exist. Maybe some day she and I will get to see one. Of course, Miss Patchy has taught me to always leave the room and go sleep under the bed whenever the doorbell rings, so I guess if a baby human ever rang the doorbell we would never see it anyway. I must think about this for a while, as it is somewhat confusing.

I have been thinking lately about going back out onto the roof sometime. That scary experience was a while ago, and that was the first time I was ever scared out there. Maybe things are okay out there now. I will think about checking it out once again. Miss

Patchy never goes out there, or maybe just a little way out. She would just rather lie down in the doorway and feel the air blow over her, or maybe see a little bit of sunshine. Now that it is hot out there, Mom and Dad never leave the door open, and there is a machine that makes a noise and blows cold air out of the walls. It's a little scary, but Miss Patchy isn't afraid of it, so I guess it's okay. She says that every year when it gets hot outside the machine blows out cold air. Also, it blows warm air out when it is cold outside, but not very often. The cold air blows out all day long. It is on, then it is off, then it is on, and so on. I guess maybe it would be too hot in the house if the cold air didn't blow out. Why is it hot outside sometimes, and sometimes cold outside? I don't really understand it. There is another thing to think about. Is my little brain capable of thinking about all these things?

Here is another puzzle. Sometimes Mom and Dad talk to a little box that they hold up to their ears. What on earth is it and why do they talk to it? I think the box talks to them, too, because sometimes they are not saying anything and then they talk again, or laugh or something. Very odd! Maybe Miss Patchy and I can figure it out some day. They often leave their little boxes lying around on a table or the couch or something. Maybe she and I can investigate them and find out how to talk to them.

Speaking of puzzles, Mom did what she calls a puzzle. It was many, many pieces of cardboard on the eating room table. They had colors on them and looked like fun toys. I went up on the table and grabbed a piece and took it down on the floor with me. It had an unusual taste and I wanted to check it out some more, but Mom got mad and took it away from me. She was upset because I pulled a lot of pieces away from where she had put them and she had to put them all back. After that, she started putting a piece of cloth on top of the "puzzle" and put other stuff on top of the cloth so I couldn't pull it off the table. Miss Patchy says that Mr. Cherokee always used to play with Mom's puzzles, but he was a lot stronger and bigger than I am and he would often take them apart. He also would sometimes pull the cloth off the puzzle. She said that Mom would get very mad at Mr. Cherokee, but he would just laugh. Miss Patchy said that she sometimes went up and checked out the puzzles, too. Somehow I just can't imagine Miss Patchy doing anything wrong, although Mom has had to tell her not to scratch on the furniture a few times lately.

Dad vacuumed yesterday. I was curious about the vacuum cleaner when I came here, but Miss Patchy told me that I should stay away from it and go rest under the bed when they turn it on. I always go with her, but I think I would like to know more about it to see what it does and why they turn it on and rub it over the floor. Hm-m-m-m-m! A very curious thing!

Well, I hear my toys calling me so I must go and play with them. One can never have too much fun!

Regards,
Mina

Feeling Better Every Day

I just had a delicious breakfast a little while ago, but haven't yet had my morning nap. I'm actually not all that tired, but I know I will be.

Mina and I have been wrestling quite a bit these days. Some days I don't mind, but other days I guess I am a little cranky and would prefer not to wrestle with her. She is wiry and strong for her size (quite small), but I am bigger and heavier, so it's a pretty even match. When I'm done, I just growl and she gets the idea pretty quickly. She learns fast.

A few days ago, Mom and Dad were sitting by the computer and he was playing with Mina, using the stick with the little pieces of cloth hanging on a string from the end. He then turned to me and I actually played with it. I didn't do the impossible acrobatic flips that Mina does, as I was lying down at the time, but it is the first time I have felt like playing for a long time. It felt good.

Mom keeps talking about jealousy between Mina and me. I know that every time I am sitting or lying next to or on either Mom or Dad, Mina will lie down somewhere that she can see us and we can see her. She will rest her head on her paws and just glare very angrily at us. I don't know how she can justify being angry about that, since she is the interloper. What right does she have to be cuddled and petted by Mom and Dad? I get angry sometimes when I see her with them, because I should be there instead of her. I'm not jealous, though, only concerned with my rights. Mina is the one who is jealous, since she is obviously inferior to me. Mom tries to get both of us up in the comfy chair with her, but that's just not acceptable to me. When Mina comes up, I go down. Just showing my displeasure with Mina's company!

Mom and Dad have been watching all the news about something called Hurricane Irene. It would appear to be something worrisome and they are afraid that Mom's daughter will suffer from it. What is it? Will it ever come to Phoenix? I hope not, because I don't think I would like it at all. They said it will bring a lot of rain and maybe flooding. That definitely would not be fun. The only water I like is what is in our water bowl, and that comes from the refrigerator. I've seen water come from the sky (rain), and it's most unpleasant. I always go into the house from the patio the instant it begins. Mom just laughs at me when I do that.

Mina has been watching television a lot lately. She will lie on the couch or on the comfy chair and stare intently at the television. She watches mostly when there are dogs or felines on the screen, but I've seen her watch humans, too. Maybe I will watch a little some time, as life occasionally gets a little boring around here. I think I know how to turn on the TV, so we could watch it while Mom and Dad are gone, too.

I think I mentioned before about Mina's curiosity getting her into a little trouble. She has spent a night outside because of it, she has had things fall on her because of it, and a number of other things. I don't think I ever said anything about what happened a little while ago. Mom was in the eating room reading or eating or something and Dad was upstairs working on the computer. Mina smelled something tasty in the food room, so she jumped up onto the counter and onto the thing they call a stove. They cook food on the stove, and sometimes they leave the pan sitting there after cooking. Well, Mina wanted to taste what was in the pan, but it was very hot and she got a little burn. Fortunately for her, she is pretty fast, so it didn't really burn her, but she was not happy about it. She jumped down very quickly and I think she will stay away from the stove from now on.

I have been lying on the table in the eating room lately. Haven't done that for a while. It is a nice view out the window. Sometimes both Mina and I are up on the table. Mom does not like it at all and makes us get down, but I take my time about it. After all, it is my house, too, why shouldn't I be able to enjoy everything in it. What's wrong with lying on the table? It's the only way I can see out the window, because I think the window sill is a little too narrow for me to fit.

Well, I feel a nap overtaking me. I must go find a comfortable place to sleep.

Yours,
Apache

Anger

I just had a much-needed nap. I was so angry this weekend that I just got really tired.

Mom and Dad got home last night. They left on Friday and just got home yesterday, on Sunday night. I was so angry with them that I didn't bother to come downstairs last night. I decided to show them! When the neighbor came over to feed us, I actually came downstairs and allowed her to pet me. Mina, on the other hand, did not show her face, but chose to greet Mom and Dad. When will she learn the proper way to act? When will Mom and Dad learn that they should never leave us? I remember when Mom decided to move to the house called Phoenix. She took Cherokee and me with her. We didn't like rolling too much in the car, but it was great to sleep with her every night, instead of comforting each other when she left us alone. Mina wasn't a lot of comfort to me. She has her toys, but she also went around the house looking for Mom and calling out for her. Silly girl! I told her what to expect and what to do, but she wouldn't listen. Now Mom and Dad know that Mina missed them and was happy to see them come home. I, on the other hand, let them know my displeasure with their disappearing act, by not coming down to greet them until this morning. What do they do when they leave the house? Anything? Or do they just sit outside somewhere and think about how else they can make me unhappy?

Mom always says that they are going to away. Where

is this away anyhow? I've tried to figure it out, but all I can think of is that it is another house somewhere. I think they sleep there, because they take pajamas. This time they took food, too, so I guess they ate there, also. I'm not sure I would like to go to away, but I guess if Mom and Dad were there, it wouldn't be too bad. At least then I would know what and where it is. All I know is they walk out the door and leave us here.

Anyway, I really am glad they're back, I just don't want them to know. The neighbor gave us just dry food. Ugh! This morning I threw it up. Mom says we need it for nutrients and to keep our teeth in good shape. It's okay when she gives us canned food and her homemade food along with the dry stuff, it's a nice variety, but just dry food is awful. I'm glad she came to her senses and started giving us wet food again, after a long while of just the dry stuff.

Mom left some nice stuff on the couch for us. There was a pillow, a blanket, and a sheet. I liked the blanket okay, but I didn't bother with the pillow, too puffy. It felt unstable. Mina likes to lie on Dad's pillow, but that's because it smells like him. I do like to curl up by Mom's bed pillow, because of her scent on it, but I don't really care about sleeping right on it.

Mina was really kissing up last night. She cried off and on for hours outside Mom and Dad's bedroom door. What a little suck-up! Once in a while, I have been resting peacefully under their bed when they have closed the door and gone to sleep. That's okay. In the morning I let them know I am there and then they let me out. Of course, Mina cries a lot, because she is all alone when I'm shut in the bedroom with them. She needs to learn that they will keep shutting her out of the bedroom until she stops playing with the chain on the wall, because it keeps Mom and Dad awake. She doesn't at all like being out of the bedroom all alone, but it is good for her sometimes. She then appreciates me more than ever. I just don't understand how she could not appreciate me all the time. After all, I teach her things, I save her from becoming fat by sharing her food, I even wrestle with her sometimes. When she does something I don't like, I hiss at her and let her know that she has gone beyond the bounds. What's not to appreciate?

Well, I'm still feeling a little angry, so I should probably take a nap. I should feel better about life after that. Such a distressing world we live in!

Yours,
Apache

Lots of Fun

Whee! I just had breakfast and I'm feeling fine! Time to play before I take a nap!

I just wanted to say how much fun I have with Miss Patchy. When we finally get Mom to get up out of bed to feed us, we run down the stairs. I usually jump over Miss Patchy at least once on the way down. If I miss, I go back up and try again. It's just so great to run up and down the steps and jump over her. Then, on the way into the food room leap over her at least once more. It's just so much fun! She doesn't seem to mind too much. Mom gives us such a great breakfast! We both eat pretty fast, but once Miss Patchy finishes up her wet food and homemade food, she pushes me out of the way so she can finish up mine, too. Fortunately, most of the time Mom is standing right there and she says "Patchy?" in a loud voice and gently nudges her back to her own dish with her foot. Once the good stuff is gone, it doesn't really matter who eats out of which dish, so I usually let Miss Patchy eat from my dish if she wants to.

Miss Patchy and I wrestle a lot, but she doesn't want to keep going for very long. She gets grumpy and starts to growl at me. What fun! I always like to see how long it takes to make her growl. Then we can switch our tails back and forth, as if we were angry, and glare at each other. I usually jump on her a few times before she gets really mad. I then move on to play with my toys. I'm always finding new ones, too. Just the other day, I found a flat, round toy on the dresser. It had a little hook-like thing on it. For some reason, it didn't play very well, so I left it on the bedroom floor. Dad picked it up and showed it to Mom who said it was an earring. She put it away in the closet.

That's another thing. When Mom and Dad were gone last week, Dad left the closet door open. It was a lot of fun playing with the things hanging down from Mom's clothes. I also cleaned off the top of the little cabinet in there, except for a few heavy things. There were more of those earrings hanging on a thing on top of the cabinet, but I couldn't get any of them off to play with. Darn! They looked like a lot of fun. Another great toy is what Mom calls twister ties. Dad almost never remembers to close the bread bags and leaves the twister ties on the counter. Of course, Mom and Dad don't want me on the counter, but I go anyway. What harm can there be in it? Anyway, I want to go on the counter, and when I do, I always grab those twister ties and play with them all over the house, although sometimes I put them in the water bowl. Mom finds them and then talks to Dad about closing the bread bags and keeping the twister ties away from me. What a spoil sport!

A couple of days ago, Dad brought home what they called a balloon. It was round and red and, at first, it hung out on the ceiling. Mom pulled it down and showed it to me. I didn't like it at all and I kept backing away from it. She tied it to a chair leg so it wouldn't go up in the high part of the couch room ceiling. The next day, it was hanging out on the floor. Mom took its string off the chair leg and bounced it around on the floor. I watched, but I still didn't like it. This morning, I don't know where it is. Maybe it ran away because I didn't like it. It seemed kind of sad, since it wasn't up by the ceiling any more.

Lately, I have been spending a lot of time in the eating room window. What wonderful things, windows. I'm not quite sure how they work, but there are a lot of things to see in a window. Sometimes there are buzz birds in the window and sometimes there are other things. Sometimes, even Mom is in the window. Hmmmm! I wonder if I could ever be in the window. Is it like the television? I've never seen a buzz bird or Mom in the television. When Mom opens the door and goes outside, I can see her in the window. I must try to get outside to see if I can get in the window. Who would see me in the window, though? I'm the one who looks at it.

I've also been watching television a lot with Mom and Dad. Sometimes I lie on the floor under the comfy chair, and sometimes I lie on the couch next to them. There are so many people and other creatures in the television. I have gone up on the cabinet that holds the television, but I can't figure out how to get into it myself. This is very puzzling. Miss Patchy says not to worry about it and to take a nice nap, but I need to figure this out. I'm a little tired now, though, so I guess I will think about it later, after a nap.

Regards,
Mina

Strange Times

I haven't yet had time to play today. I just finished breakfast a short time ago and had to take a little nap before playing. I lay in the office window and slept off breakfast.

I would like to tell about something strange that happened the other night. We were all sitting in the couch room, watching television. I can't remember what was on, but I think it was just changing all the time, the way it does sometimes when Dad has the little box in his hand. Anyway, we were just sitting there and Mom and Dad were talking, when all the lights went out. The television went out, too, and the ceiling fans stopped. It was a little scary, but Miss Patchy and I could see okay. I'm not sure about Mom and Dad. Dad stayed on the couch, and Mom walked slowly into the food room. When she came out of the food room, she had some sort of a stick in her hand. When she made the stick click, light came out of it. It made a little circle of light on the floor, or on the wall, or wherever it settled. When Mom got back to the couch room, she lit a candle and there was some light in the room then. I found it all very odd. Why didn't they just turn on the lights and the television? There must have been some sort of reason why.

After a few minutes of sitting in the light of the candle, Mom told Dad that she was going to go upstairs on the roof to see if everybody's lights were off. The little circle of light from the light stick went up with her. I ran up after her and managed to dash out onto the roof before Mom could stop me. It was very exciting! There was a really bright light coming down from the sky. Who needed lights? Mom looked around and said that everybody's lights were off except for some way off, where she could see some lights. I couldn't see, because of the wall. I was going to go up on the wall to see what I could see, but Mom grabbed me and took me back inside before I could do so.

We went back downstairs and Mom and Dad talked some more. Mom said they might as well go to bed, since they couldn't watch television or read or anything. She said they could talk in the dark in bed just as well as in the dark in the couch room. It had been dark for quite a while by then, so they went upstairs and got ready for bed. Mom turned off the switches on the cords in the office, turned off the cold air machine, and turned on the light switch for the shower light. They weren't in bed for long before the shower light came on. Mom got up and turned on the cold air machine and turned off the shower light and the two of them went to sleep.

Why did the lights go off? Will I ever find out? Did Mom or Dad do something? Why were all the lights off when Mom looked around from the roof? Where does the light come from anyway? All I know is that someone clicks a switch on the wall and there is light. I have asked Miss Patchy, but she doesn't know either. She also said she didn't really care, just as long as there is light and she is comfortable and gets good food. I certainly appreciate all those things, but I am really curious about the missing lights. Mom said something about electricity and power. I don't know what that is, but it must have something to do with the lights. I guess I will have to let it go for now, since no one seems to be able to explain it to me.

Another strange thing happened yesterday. I found the balloon. It didn't run away after all. It was just hiding, probably embarrassed because it was getting small. It looked as though it might be fun to play with since it was smaller, so I jumped on it, intending to pick it up. Well, it made a loud noise and turned into a little piece of plastic. That scared me. What happened? Another mysterious event! The world is just full of strange, unexplainable things. Dad threw what was left of the balloon in the garbage, along with the string that was attached to it. Maybe another balloon will come to visit us some day.

Mom got mad at me yesterday. She went into the office in the morning and found that I had pulled a skirt off a hanger. She has several things hanging on a hook on the door. I just can't resist her clothes. Also, it's fun to make her mad. Anyway, she picked up the skirt and looked it over carefully to make sure I hadn't put any holes in it and then put it back on the hanger, saying that she must iron it. What is ironing? Maybe I will find out soon, if she irons the skirt.

Well, I think I hear my toys calling me to play. I'll just finish a short nap first and then be off.

Regards,
Mina

Curiouser and Curiouser

Well, I had a nice night, even though I slept through most of it. We had a great breakfast, and I will be playing soon, although I need a little rest first.

A new thing happened to me the other day. I was just minding my own business and looking around for something to do when I began to cough and I felt something in my throat. It was a little odd feeling, so I tried to ask Mom about it, but she didn't seem to understand what I was asking, even though she knew it was a question. I coughed a little more, and suddenly, something came up my throat, out of my mouth, and fell onto the floor. I was very surprised. I had seen Miss Patchy do that, but it had never happened to me before. I asked Miss Patchy about it and she said that I shouldn't worry; it was just a hairball. I asked her why it happened, and she explained to me that I have been shedding, with lots of my beautiful, long fur loosening up. I have been having to groom myself a lot lately, and she said that I have been swallowing my fur for a long time and now it was time for it to come up. She said it happens pretty often and that now I am an adult it will probably happen a lot. No more kitten, even though I still feel quite kittenish. Mom says I play like a kitten, too. Why do I have to be an adult? Actually, though, I don't really see any difference except that I now have hairballs. At least it doesn't hurt!

The lights went off again, just a few days after the last time. It was daytime, so we didn't need the light stick or the candles. Later on, Mom said that a car had hit a utility pole (whatever that is) and that turned our lights off. What does a car hitting this pole have to do with our lights? They weren't off for very long, which Mom said was good because it was pretty hot outside and the cold air machine didn't work, either. I'm glad it hasn't happened at our meal time, because Mom says we shouldn't open the refrigerator when the lights are out, so that it won't warm up inside. Our food is in there! It's scary to think that we might not be able to eat because the lights go out.

Dad has been going away every day for a few days now. He says that he has a job and has to go away to it. It's very lonely here when both Mom and Dad are gone. Mom has a job, too, but she goes away mostly in the morning, while Dad goes away in the afternoon and evening, so most of the time we are not alone. When Dad is home, he spends a lot of time on the computer, so I go up to the office to help him. Sometimes I watch him from the second chair, sometimes I watch him from on top of the desk. Sometimes he plays with me and sometimes he strokes me. I like Dad a lot. I like Mom, too, because she is also very good at stroking me. They both spend too much time stroking Miss Patchy, though. Sometimes I get a little mad and just lie there and glare at them while they are stroking her. I'm not sure they even notice me. I always feel as though I shouldn't let them stroke me any more when they do that, but then they start doing it and I have to let them.

Mom cooked some food for Miss Patchy and me last night. I heard her tell Dad that there is chicken, beef kidney, and chicken hearts, gizzards and liver in it. It smelled very good, but I would rather eat the dry food. Miss Patchy would rather eat the wet food and the stuff Mom cooks, so we often exchange our dishes. The whole house smelled really good, and Dad was hungry when he came home from work and he ate some of our chicken. It takes Mom quite a while to make the food. She cooks it for a long time, then lets it cool off, and then she has to chop it up. She mixes some of the cooking juice with it and then puts it in little containers that she keeps in the freezer. She is a very good Mom and Dad is a very good Dad, because he gives us treats. While our food was cooking, he took a chicken heart out of the pot and chopped it up and gave it to us. I liked that.

Well, it is getting late in the morning and I haven't played yet. Lots of playing to do, lots of toys to play with. So many toys, so little time!

Regards,
Mina

Am I Growing Up?

It's so nice to be awake these days. Miss Patchy insists on sleeping a lot, even though I try to get her to play. She does play a little sometimes and it is fun. Now, when Mom opens the windows and the patio doors, a lot of cold comes in. Before, it was hot, but now it's cold. I just can't figure out why that changes. Miss Patchy says it happens all the time. Anyway, it is so cold at night that both Miss Patchy and I often sleep on the bed to keep Mom and Dad's feet warm. We also just snuggle up together during the day and keep each other warm while we nap. I am doing a lot more napping during the day now. What does that mean? I have also been spending a good bit of time alone, lying in the office window or in one of the office chairs. I never used to want to be alone, but life seems to be changing.

Well, I think I have finally figured out the window! I saw Dad open the door and go outside. I immediately jumped up on the window sill, and there he was in the window. I had sort of noticed this before, but I have realized that it is some sort of hole in the wall, with a clear barrier over it. I wondered before if I could be in the "television" (actually a window), and I think that I am in it when I am up on the window sill. Mom and Dad can see me when they are outside and I am looking through the window. I know that they can see me, because they talk to me. I guess you can see through it from both sides! There are so many amazing things in life. Will I ever learn about them all?

Mom and Dad are very worried about money right now. I'm not even sure what money is, but I'm glad I don't have to worry about it, or anything else. Mom says that money is what gives us food to eat and a roof over our heads. However, I see Mom make our food, so I'm not sure what she is talking about. This "money" has never been at the stove cooking our food, as far as I have ever seen. Is money a person? Is it fun to play with?

I was told by Mom a little while ago that I am now one year old. Hm-m-m-m! Just what does that mean? She says that Miss Patchy is about twelve or thirteen years old. Why does Miss Patchy have more years than I? Mom says that she (Mom) is retired, because she is old. How old is she? What does retired mean? Will I have to retire some day? I remember Mom and Dad talking about getting new tires for the car. (I think that's the thing that takes us to the vet.) Did the car retire? This is puzzling to me. Miss Patchy doesn't seem to know the answer, either, and she says she doesn't really care about it. Sometimes she is very curious, but other times not at all.

Mom says that she gets Social Security now. I don't know what that is, but she is glad to have it. Will I get it when I am old? Miss Patchy says that she does not get Social Security. I thought she would be old enough for it, but she says not.

Closets are not my friends. I just can't resist going into closets, but bad things often happen when I do. I think I told you (or Miss Patchy told you) about my experience in the coat closet when I was very little. After that, I always let Mom know when I was going into the coat closet. When I got shut in the garage for a long time, I started letting Mom know when I was going out there, and made a little game of it, just daring her to catch me and take me back inside the house. Well, I love to go into the clothes closet off the bedroom and bathroom upstairs. It is full of Mom's fun clothing. She has a lot of clothes with things hanging off them. I just love to play with *them. Mom hates it when I do that, so she always keeps the clothes closet shut so I can't go in. Well, the other day, I pushed on the door, and it opened. I went in and had some fun and then went to sleep. When Mom got home from work, she came upstairs and changed her clothes in the closet. She was surprised to see that the closet door was open and she looked around for me, but didn't see me. When she was done changing, she left the closet and shut the door. Oh-oh! I couldn't get out. For a long time I tried and tried to get the door open or to get out some other way, but there just was no other way. I got a little scared and panicky and I tried to climb up the door on Mom's housecoats. One came off and fell on the floor. I climbed a little way up the other one, but there was no way out by going up. Then, I tried to dig my way out under the door. I got the edge of the carpet up and pulled it inside the closet, but the opening was too small for me, and there were sharp things there. I heard Mom and Dad calling me, but I couldn't answer loud enough for them to hear me, because they were watching television. Finally, when I didn't come down for supper (I always do!), Mom looked all around and finally found me in the closet. I will have to be sure to let her know when I go in there now, so she doesn't shut me in again.*

I know some toys that need to be played with now, so I will end for today. I hope that you will enjoy your toys, too.

Regards,
Mina

Opposable Thumbs

I have been napping quite a bit lately, mostly to keep warm. I even welcome Mina's proximity, since she has some heat to share. It is mutual, I guess.

Anyway, to get to my subject. Opposable thumbs are highly touted, but I think perhaps they are highly overrated, too. Mom used to tease Cherokee and me about not having opposable thumbs. She would show us how she could pick up things and then laugh a little at us because we couldn't do that. Well, we have sharp claws and sharp teeth that do a pretty good job of picking things up, believe me. No, we can't pick up a book or a piece of furniture, but they would be too heavy for us anyway. Also, why would we want to pick up those particular things? They are of no importance to us. Well, maybe a little importance, as we do sleep on the furniture and occasionally we do read, but we have no reason to pick up anything like that.

Lately, Mom has been complaining that her wonderful opposable thumbs are hurting a lot, because she picks up a lot of heavy law books in her job. I don't know what law books are, but she says they are very heavy, as books go. She has to pick up a lot of them with her wonderful opposable thumbs when she is at work, and now those very same wonderful opposable thumbs are hurting and she doesn't like to pick things up much right now. Ha! So much for opposable thumbs! Now she is pretty helpless, since she doesn't have sharp claws or sharp teeth. Are felines superior, or what!

Actually, we do have a little bit of a thumb-like appendage on each paw, but they just don't work quite like human thumbs. They are not long enough to be very useful for things other than scratching something or someone. At that they do a nice job. Unfortunately, Mom and Dad get mad when we scratch stuff with those claws or any other claws. They just spoil all the fun in life.

I have been spending a lot of nights sleeping on the bed with Mom and Dad. I usually end up being shut in the room with them, because Mina can't manage to behave herself and keeps playing with their feet, or getting up on the dresser and knocking the big chain against the wall, so they throw her out and shut the door. She doesn't like to sleep all night, because she just wants to play. Well, too bad for her! I love sleeping with them. Cherokee wasn't much for sleeping all night, either, but he would just leave the bedroom and play somewhere else, except for the last couple of years. Then he would sleep peacefully at Mom's feet every night.

Right now, I'm a little worried about Mom. She smells funny and all I want to do is stay close to her to help keep her safe. The smell seems to be coming from one of her milk holders. I kept nudging at it to try to let her know that there was something wrong. I don't know what's going on, but she has been telling me that she will be fine. She tells me that she will go to the hospital (whatever that is) and when she comes home she will be just fine. Can I believe her? I hope so. I don't want to lose Mom. I'm sure life with just Dad would be great, but I have been with Mom for a very long time, and I think that maybe losing Mom would be worse than losing Cherokee, if that is possible. I will continue to worry about

Mom until she can prove to me that she is fine. We will find out next week.

What is a hospital anyway? I have not heard of that before. Is it a place, a home? I don't know why Mom has to go to one, as we have a home right here. What do people do at a hospital? Mina says she doesn't know, but she is young yet and there are a lot of things she doesn't know. I will have to find out more about this hospital.

Well, I'm tired again. This cold weather just takes it all out of me and I find I must nap a lot.

Yours,
Apache

Mom

Nothing like a nice nap on Mom's lap! Absolutely the best!

I've been very worried about Mom for some time now. There was a sort of funny smell to her and I stayed with her wherever she went in the house and always, always slept on her lap when she sat down. Sometimes I even braved the closed bedroom door to sleep on the bed with her, or just to be near her. I just felt that something was not quite right.

Finally, she went to see a vet, or as she calls it, a doctor. She came back smelling even odder, so I stuck by her some more. She said they poked a hole in her. Awful!! I certainly would not want anyone to poke a hole in me! Why would they do that? Does it let out the bad smell?

Last week, she went to a place called a hospital for the day and came back smelling even stranger, if that's possible. However, the first funny smell seems to be gone. She has been wearing some unusual pieces of clothing (as if they all weren't strange!), but I stayed with her. The smell seemed to come from her left milk holder and the under part of the arm near it. I smelled both those places thoroughly and then rubbed against them and curled up on them to keep her warm. I purred to help her heal. I think it is working. Mom says that she really appreciates all I do for her and loves it when I come up in her lap and do the purr cure, and says that she is healing very well.

Please, Mom! Don't leave me. I need you. I love Dad, and I even am fond of Mina, but I love Mom the most, since I have known her for so long. What would I do without her? It was bad enough losing Cherokee, but I would not survive losing Mom, too. Mom keeps telling me that she is going to be just fine, that they took all the bad stuff out and she is healing well and will be as good as new very soon. She says that she still needs to do more stuff to be sure she will stay okay for the rest of her life. Will there be new strange smells? I will keep purring the cure as long as it takes to make her healed and well.

I don't think Mina has even noticed the smells. She spends more time with Dad and certainly hasn't known Mom as long as I. Of course, she would miss Mom, but she would get over it before long, especially if she had Dad. She is young and is still capable of handling all sorts of things. I, on the other hand, am not. I am no longer flexible, either in my mind or in my body. Maybe if I lost a little weight . . .

Mom got up real early this morning to go see the vet/doctor, and she says she has to get up even earlier tomorrow – something about a balloon. I think Mina had a balloon once. I just can't figure out what a balloon has to do with Mom's milk holder. Perhaps I heard incorrectly. I also heard another new word from her – radiation. What is it? Mom says she is afraid of it, but feels she must do it (whatever it is). I guess maybe we shall see.

Well, I think it's time for another nap, once I have finished eating my supper. Dad is home and will be feeding us soon.

Yours,
Apache

Holidays

Well, the holidays are over. At least, that's what Mom says. I'm not really sure exactly what a holiday is, but there is usually a lot of good food. Also, Mom doesn't have to work on holidays, although she used to. I have never worked on holidays. Of course, I have never worked. At least not that I'm aware of. Anyway, now Dad has to work on holidays. Dad finally got a job! He was very depressed about not having one, although I can't imagine even wanting one, but he's human – what can you expect? He works at some place called Papa John's and he has to work a lot at night, on weekends and on holidays. We would rather have him at home on those days.

I am told that Thanksgiving is the name of one holiday. It is probably my favorite of all of them, because we have turkey to eat. I love turkey. It is my favorite bird! I like chicken a lot, but turkey is even better. This year Mom saved the dark meat (neither she nor Dad like it) and cooked some other stuff, like livers and things, and mixed in the turkey's dark meat. She froze most of it and we ate it for a long time. It is only just now running out, so Mom had to cook some more food yesterday. It smelled wonderful in here.

I like Christmas, too. Mom used to bring a tree into the house for Christmas. It was a little bit scary, though. She would hang things on it and it would be really sparkly. Cherokee and I used to lie down under it, on the white sheet she put there. I guess it was supposed to look like snow, but who likes snow? I sure don't; it's cold! Back in Malden, Mom would let us out on the back porch on cold, snowy days, and that stuff was just freezing. After a couple of minutes, we would run back into the house and try to get warm, and lick the water off our paws. Ugh! Snow! I haven't seen any at this house, even though it is sometimes a little cold.   One time, there were some little white balls piled up out on the patio. Mom called it hail. I didn't like that, either. It was cold, too.

Anyway, the first year Dad was here, he and Mom had a tree in the house. Last year and this year, though, they decided not to, because Mom was just too tired to decorate it. Also, Mom said that trees are very expensive here. I kind of hope they have one again, because it smells nice and reminds me of the woods where I was born. Feline mother, where are you now? They did put up lights outside, but I didn't see them. I just heard them talking about the lights. There were also things around the house, like little candle things on what Mom called a sleigh. Just before Mom put the Christmas things away, Mina stole one of the little candle things. Even I don't know where it is. Mom says that we will find it the next time we move.

Another reason I like Christmas is because Santa Claus brings things to us in our stocking. I have never seen him, but Mom says that he is fat and wears a red suit with white trim. He is supposed to come down the chimney, but we don't have one. Dad says that she shouldn't talk to us about Santa, because he thinks that it's wrong to try to make us believe in Santa. Whatever! All I care about is what is left in our stocking, no matter who puts it there. This year, we got two cans of sardines, two cans of tuna, and two pouches of treats. Um-m-m-m-m! Treats! Mina loves them, too, so we always have a little struggle when Dad opens up the pouch.

Mom and Dad stayed up until midnight on what they call New Year's Eve. They watched some silly thing on TV where people were yelling and shouting and singing. Mom and Dad kissed each other and not long after, they went to bed. Mom cooked corned beef for New Year's Day, but she wouldn't give us any, saying that it wasn't good for us - too much salt and seasoning. It smelled pretty good, though, and Dad did sneak us a couple of little bits of it.

Last week was another holiday, for Mom, anyway. She said that banks and government offices were closed, and some other places, too. I don't know what all those places are, except that banks are where we get money from, but she didn't have to work, so she was able to stay home with us again. It was Martin Luther King, Jr.'s birthday. Mom was sorry that he hadn't been born in March, so that the holidays could be spread out a little. Now there won't be another holiday for a long time. It doesn't really matter to me, since (as I mentioned before) I don't work anyway. The main reason I like some holidays is because of the food.

Well, I'm a little tired and think I should take a nap before supper. It wouldn't do to be too tired to eat!

Yours,
Apache

More Worries About Mom

Well, neither Mina nor I have written for some time, as you can tell. I have been incredibly worried about Mom. For a long time, she has had trouble walking, and it hurt her a lot. She used a stick (she called it a cane) to help her get around. Sometimes she would cry because it hurt so much.

Well, one morning, before it even got light, she and Dad left the house. They fed us first, of course. Dad came back later that night to feed us, but then he went away again and we didn't see him until morning. This went on for a few days, just seeing him in the morning and at night, when he came to feed us. He didn't even sleep here. We didn't see Mom at all. I was very scared, and so was Mina. We just couldn't understand where she was.

Finally, a few days later, Dad brought Mom home. She had to push a thing called a walker around, but she smiled a lot and said that her hip didn't hurt any more. I was glad to hear that, but why did she have to push that thing around? One day a woman called a nurse (whatever that is) came to the house, and another day, a man that Mom called a Physical Therapist came to the house. Mom slept on the couch a lot and didn't get up much, and she kept on pushing that walker thing around. How weird! Sometimes she stuck herself in the stomach with a metal claw, and she took some pills.

The next week, the Physical Therapist man came again, twice. He made Mom do some exercise things, and she started walking with her stick again, and she started going upstairs, too. We were so glad to have her back home, but she smelled real funny. Even she noticed it. One day she said she wasn't going to take any more pills, because they made her sick. Another day, she said she wasn't going to stick herself in the stomach any more, either, because it made her heart pound at night.

On Monday of the next week, Dad took Mom to work. She took just her cane. Boy! Was she tired when she came home! She slept for a long time after that. She worked again on Tuesday, but then not again until Thursday. Actually, that's her regular schedule. She was happy to be back at work, but it still made her very tired. One day, Dad took her to the store. That made her tired, too. Well, I guess I can sympathize with that! Most things make me tired; that's why I take naps all the time. Eating is tiring, running up and down the steps is tiring, sometimes even sleeping is tiring. Mina doesn't get nearly as tired as I do, but she is so young yet.

But I digress. Mom started going somewhere else to see the Physical Therapist man, although I guess it was a woman where she went. Sometimes she was a little sore the next day, but almost every day she did more and more stuff. Driving herself around was the next step, and then walking to the store. That really tired her out!

Anyway, Mom says she got a total hip replacement on her left side. I'm not sure what a hip is, and I'm not sure I have any, but Mom does. Her hip doesn't hurt any more, she smiles a lot, and now she walks most of the time without her cane. She says she is going to sell it when she is sure she no longer needs it. I will be glad to see it gone, and Mina will, too. One day in the food room, Mina got in the way and the cane accidentally hit her on the head. Mom felt just terrible and tried to comfort Mina, but she can't bend over yet, so she couldn't really reach Mina. I know that she wouldn't hurt anyone, especially one of us or Dad.

We are all so happy to have Mom home. She has started cooking and baking again, although not nearly as much as before, at least not yet. She says that she will have to make us some more food soon, and maybe it will be fish this time. There is a sale on whole, frozen fish somewhere, and she says she wants to buy it and cook it with some other stuff for us. I hope it will be as good as the chicken food she cooks. Yum!!!

Well, just thinking about eating has made me very tired. I guess it is time to take a nap.

Yours,
Apache

Doors

Wow! What a great time playing! I have a rattly ball, and it is just so much fun! I need to calm down a little now and try to work some things out.

I've been pretty busy studying things lately, so I really haven't had time to put my thoughts onto this blog. I am very, very curious about doors. Doors are what let people into and out of rooms. Rooms are big empty spaces, surrounded by walls, where humans put tables and chairs and other things. Doorways are empty places in the walls so that people can go in and out of the rooms. Most doorways have doors that cover them so that, when they are closed, people cannot go in or out. So far, so good! I've had quite a bit of experience with doors, not all of it good. I think I mentioned the time when Mom and Dad went away all day, and I was shut in the closet. I always try to be sure that Mom sees me go into the closet now so that she will leave the door open a little for me, so I can get out when I am ready. She doesn't understand why I love to go into the closet, but to me it is a dark and mysterious place, with lots of boxes and nice-smelling things.

There is also the door into the garage. It is different from the other doors. It is a little bit ugly and it makes a different sound when it shuts. It sounds heavy. It is always exciting to go into the garage to check out all the things that are kept in there. Mom and Dad used to keep the car in the garage, but the big door that slides up to the ceiling no longer works, so they can't get the car in or out. That makes it much better for me, since the car is just a little bit scary. I don't mind it at first when the door is closed after I go into the garage, but they always turn out the light, too, and then I get a little afraid and want to go back into the house. If Mom and Dad are watching TV, they sometimes don't hear me calling them to come let me back into the house. Now I always try to let them know that I have gone out into the garage so they know where I am.

There are also the glass doors in the couch room that let me out onto the patio. They are like windows. I can see outside, but I can't get there unless Mom or Dad slides open one of the glass doors and that thing they call a screen. There are more glass doors in the guest room, but they are almost never open. It's funny to be looking out the guest room doors and see Mom or Miss Patchy in the couch room, through those glass doors.

Here is what I don't understand about doors. When I want to go into the bedroom or the guest room, maybe the bathroom, if the door is just open a little bit, I can lift up my front legs, push on the door, and it opens up and I go into the room. Sometimes, I find something interesting behind the door, and it closes a little bit, with not quite enough room for me to get out. So, I lift my front legs, push on the door, and instead of opening, it closes and latches so that I can't get out. Why doesn't pushing on the door work all the time? Both Mom and Miss Patchy tell me that I'm doing it wrong, that I can't push the door open from the inside. But what else can I do? This will take a lot more study on my part. I can see that I have a lot to learn yet. Will I ever be as wise as Miss Patchy? She sleeps a lot and eats a lot, and I don't think she can see really well anymore, but she is still smart and wise, but most of the time she won't share that wisdom with me.

Windows still confuse me, too. I have been investigating and studying, but I'm still not sure I have all the answers. Sometimes, when Mom comes home, I will be in the eating room window and I *see her on the walkway. She wiggles her fingers at me and puts her finger to my nose, but I can't feel it or smell it. All I can do is see it. I already learned that a window cannot be used like a door. I tried, but I can't get through it, even though I can see stuff on the other side. Sort of like the glass doors, I guess. It is a puzzle I will have to think about for a while.*

Well, there are some toys waiting for my attention. I wouldn't want them to be lonely, so I must go play with them. So much responsibility! I will continue to think about doors and windows, to see if I can figure them out.

Regards,
Mina

Does Mom Love Miss Patchy More?

Whew! It's time to rest a little after jumping for birds and bugs out on the patio. I love it out there and ask Mom every day to let me go out. Most of the time it's either too cold or too hot and she doesn't want to keep the door open. Sometimes early in the morning she will let us out, before it gets really hot. She won't open the door at all once it gets hot.

Mom loves Miss Patchy more than me. I know this. I can hear. She calls Miss Patchy Pretty Girl or Beautiful Girl. She calls me Cute Girl or Cutie Girl. Why does she call me something different? I want to be Pretty Girl or Beautiful Girl, like Miss Patchy! Mom knows how I feel, because she says that I lie on the back of the comfy chair and glare at her and Miss Patchy when she is using those names. What is cute or cutie? She never uses those names for Miss Patchy, which must mean that she thinks I am not as good or nice. I know this!

Also, she always calls Miss Patchy Good Girl. So often, she calls me Bad Girl. I can tell by her tone of voice that Bad Girl is not a good thing, but Good Girl is. I laughed last week, when the perfect Miss Patchy was lying on the eating room table. Mom saw her and called her Bad Girl and told her to get down. Ha! Evidently Mom noticed how I felt about these names, and she is actually calling me Good Girl a lot. It makes me feel so good and makes me want to do the right things. Now if I could just keep myself from jumping up on the food-room counter. Mom and Dad hate when I do that, but who can resist? It smells so good up there and sometimes I find food there. Most of the time, it's human food, and nothing that I like at all, but I usually taste it and sometimes I push it over the edge to the floor so I can play with it. I tried with the things Mom calls chocolate chip cookies. I pushed them to the floor, but they just broke. I tried a lot of them, but got the same result. Finally, I gave up. Some human food makes great toys! Of course, almost anything can be a toy, especially if it is round.

Anyway, Mom has sometimes recently called me Pretty Girl. I'm really excited that maybe she really means it. She has noticed that I don't glare at her and Miss Patchy so much anymore. She has also noticed that I purr again. She has told me how much she loved it when I was little and would hug her, knead her neck, and purr a lot. When she started calling me Bad Girl when I did stuff, I stopped doing that to her. I was angry! Now that she is treating me a little better, I am purring for her again. Will I ever hug her again? I don't know. My feelings were very hurt. Miss Patchy says that I am taking things all wrong. She says that Mom loves me just as much, just in a different way. Why should she love me differently from Miss Patchy? She says that it's because we are different, but so what! I love Mom and Dad so much, and I want them to love me just as much as they love Miss Patchy. Will that ever happen? Why do I have to work so hard for it? Miss Patchy says it's because I am so young and have so much to learn. She says that being cute is wonderful and that I should be proud of it. She says that she will never be called cute, because she sleeps most of the time and doesn't do much playing at all. She's just old! She's pretty cranky sometimes, too.

These days, any time I do something right (the way Mom wants it done), she (and Dad, too) calls me Good Girl. It sounds so good to my little ears. All I want is to hear those names, not Cute Girl or Cutie Girl, or Bad Girl. Miss Patchy says that Mom and Dad think I look so cute when I play and jump around and that's why they call me that. Well, I don't care! I don't want to hear it! Let Miss Patchy hear it if she will ever get up off her lazy butt and play. Playing is life! What else can there possibly be? Well, there is Pretty Girl and Beautiful Girl, isn't there. And Good Girl! The more I hear those words, the happier I feel and the more love I feel for Mom and Dad.

Well, now that I have ranted about this, I feel a little better. I guess I should go play some more before I take a nap. I will play a lot, as long as Mom and Dad don't call me Cute Girl!

Regards,
Mina

Buttered Fingers?

I just woke up – a nap not nearly long enough! Oh well, to work!

I think that Mom's last hospital stay must have done something to her mind. She says that she had another hip replacement. I think I mentioned that before, and wasn't sure if I have a hip. I guess Mom has two of them, since she has had two replaced. I wonder if there are more. I mean, she has ten fingers and ten toes, why not more than two hips?

Anyway, since Mom came home from the hospital all smelly again, she's been eating very strange things. She had a bag with, of all things, buttered fingers in it. I have never heard of anyone eating fingers before, but I suppose it wouldn't be all that bad, except that I smelled these so-called buttered fingers, and they don't smell at all edible. Something is not quite right here, I think. I would never think of eating fingers belonging to Mom or Dad, but probably if a human were lying dead on the floor and there was nothing else to eat, I might try to eat the fingers. However, on examining fingers closely, I have found that there does not appear to be much meat on them – they're kind of skinny and bony. Mom claims to love them, though. The smell they give off is sort of like that chocolate stuff that both Mom and Dad eat. Would someone cook fingers in butter and cover them with chocolate? How odd! They are crunchy, though, so perhaps the bones are cooked to a very tender state. Hm-m-m-m! I'll have to think about this for a while, but I don't think I will be eating them anytime soon.

Humans do eat a lot of strange things, though. Mom sometimes makes something called "sloppy joes." What? Just because someone named Joe is not very neat, we are supposed to eat him? I don't think it smells like human meat, but rather beef perhaps, but there are so many other smells mixed in that I'm really not sure. I think Mom said that there are tomatoes or something in it, along with relish and maybe some other yucky things. It's something I would never eat, that's for sure. Anything that smells that bad will never pass my lips.

Mom also told me that in some places they eat something called "Toad in the Hole." I'm not exactly sure what a toad is, but I think I remember something from when I was very small. It was an ugly little thing that smelled bad, and peed on everything. Some of our people did eat them when there was nothing else, but I don't think I ever tasted it. Some humans seem to have very bad taste in food. A toad? In a hole? What is the hole made of? Can a hole actually be made of anything? Doesn't a hole have to be in something else, and not a thing on its own? Sometimes I think I will never understand humans.

Mom has also been eating celery with cream cheese. The cream cheese is okay, but celery? How many inedible things can humans think of to eat? Celery is green – I never eat green food. Celery is full of stringy stuff – I never eat stringy stuff. As I said, the cream cheese is okay. I would eat that, and Mom could have the celery.

Another thing humans eat is potatoes. What's with potatoes, anyway? I've smelled them and they smell like dirt most of the time. Humans take off the outsides of the potatoes most of the time, but not always. They are kind of white inside and they are very crispy sometimes. I have seen Mom fry them, boil them, bake them, add them to other things, and eat all of them. Dad likes them, too. What's to like? They don't have much taste, unlike fish or chicken or beef or turkey or so many other fine foods. I guess I'll just stick with meat, since it's so tasty and makes my tummy happy.

Well, I think it's nap time again, unless it's time to eat. I'll have to check my system clock and get back to myself on that.

Yours,
Apache

Chaos

I'm just up from my nap, and feel the need to get on with this blog. As I'm sure you've noticed, neither of us has written anything for a very long time. All has been chaos in our house, at least as I understand that word.

Neither Mina nor I have been able to understand much of what has been going on. Shortly after Mom had her second hip replacement, Mom and Dad decided that we would have to move – again! Where to this time, I wondered. In order to move, they decided that they must sell everything, except us and their clothes. So, once Mom was feeling okay, she began to sort things out. This was all interrupted by Mom and Dad going away – again! They left the house one morning and didn't come back for nearly a week. The neighbor came in to feed us again, and to clean our litter box. Did they think of us while they were gone? Did they go somewhere, or just stay out of the house for that week?

When they got back, they talked about something called a reunion, a cemetery, old friends, old houses, and other things, including a beach, whatever those things are. They talked about eating some places and driving around. I'm glad I didn't go, since I would much rather take a nap.

Of course, the sorting began again, and Mom began to set things up in the garage. She set up the folding tables and put a lot of stuff on them. She kept finding more and more stuff to put in the garage, until you could hardly move in there. She got really tired doing all of that, but she kept on going, until there was no longer any room for anything. Finally, the day came when the door to the garage was constantly open, our litter box and food and water dishes were upstairs, and a lot of people came into the house and were looking around. This went on for two days! When it was over, things apparently went back to normal. But not quite! A lot of things were gone that had been in the house before. Even some of the furniture was missing. The curio cabinet and the entertainment center had disappeared some time before, when someone came to take them away. Were people stealing our stuff?

There were a few more days of that type of activity, but things remained pretty much the same, until one day some people came and took away the couch, the liquor cabinet, the bedroom set, and the wonderful computer desk and one of the office chairs. That was a shock! Mom went out one day and came back with a tiny little thing to put the computer on and things were a little difficult for a while. A while after that, the garage was open most of the time, and people came and took stuff away. Mom packed away the china and a lot of other things, and taped up the boxes. It was getting really scary. Mina and I had no idea what was happening. We just stayed close to Mom and Dad and tried to keep warm and comfortable on what was left of the furniture. They moved the mattress and springs from the bed down into the couch room so they would have something to sit on, so we often cuddle there.

One day, when it was pretty cold, Mom went away. She was gone for a few days and then came back. She said that her sister-in-law had died and she had to go to the funeral. I'm not sure what that is, but she was sad for a while. She said it was an expense she hadn't needed, but she had needed to go; it was important. She said it was very cold where she had been, but it hadn't bothered her too much. She said that was a good thing, considering what they were going to do.

Oh, I'm getting so tired! I think I need a nap.

Yours,
Apache

Where to, and When?

Well, I have had a good nap, so I can continue with our adventures.

Finally, one day, Dad was in the garage, giving stuff to people who gave him pieces of paper, when Dad brought home something behind the car that he called a trailer. They started putting the taped up boxes in it, and when it was starting to get dark, Mom made us get into our boxes and put us in the car! We were getting seriously frightened by then. Some people came, gave Dad some more pieces of paper and took the rest of the stuff out of the garage. He closed the garage door and locked up the house. He and Mom got into the car (which was stuffed to the ceiling with things, including us), and off we rolled. It was like being in a closet or something. Mina and I were facing each other, but there were all kinds of things covering our boxes. It had already been dark for a while, so we didn't roll for very long. We stopped so Mom and Dad could eat something, and then we rolled on for a little while. Then we stopped and slept in a little house with just a bedroom and a bathroom. It was nice to be out of the boxes, but it was a strange place that didn't smell like home. We snuggled with Mom and Dad.

In the morning, they put us back into our boxes and we rolled off again! We continued to roll all day long. I was not too scared, as I had done this before, when Cherokee and I moved with Mom from Malden to Phoenix. Mina, however, was quite concerned. She couldn't understand being shut up in her box for so long. I told her to just go to sleep, and she would wake up when it was time to get out of the box. We both slept, and went into another little house called Texas. It was quite late in the day already.

The next day was a repeat of the previous day, but this time the house was called Austin. Mom and Dad left us in the strange place all evening, and went to her nephew's house, where they ate a wonderful dinner. We just had dry food! The house we were in was very old and not in very good condition. Mom said that the only thing good about it was that it was cheap. Again, we spent only one night there.

On the following day, Mom said that they had to change their plans. They wanted to go see her sister in Florida, but she said it was way too hard on Mina and me to keep going for so many days in the car. Yes!!! Finally, she was thinking of us! She said that we would turn north and head straight for Massachusetts. Massachusetts? Didn't we leave that house once, a long time ago? Anyway, we got into the car again and that night we spent in a little house called Arkansas. Mom said there had been an accident on the freeway and the traffic was stopped. They decided not to go on to Memphis, and we stayed in the little house right by the freeway. It was much better than the house called Austin. I was really going stir crazy, and had to see out the window or die! Mom helped me to get into the window, behind the curtains, and I stayed there for a long time, just dreaming of freedom and maybe being home again. Mina was just trying to get attention all night and woke Mom up. Dad spent some time on the computer, since the house had something called free WI FI. Neither one of them slept very much.

The traffic was much better the next day, and we reluctantly got into the boxes. Mina fought very hard against it, but I told her it was useless. Mom and Dad are bigger than we are, and they will always win! Mom kept saying that a storm was coming and that we needed to keep ahead of it. She thought maybe it would not come quite as far as we were, but we kept on rolling. When we stopped, we stayed in a little house called Ohio. All of the little houses were pretty much the same, mostly just different colors. I really didn't like them much, but they were better than being in the car.

When we went to the car the next morning, it was pretty cold and I was shivering. Mina complained of the cold, too. She made a big show of not getting into the box this morning. She hid behind a piece of furniture and Dad had to pull some drawers out so he could get to her. She was pretty mad, but after the car warmed up and we were ready to sleep, she calmed down. What else could she do? Mom said it snowed a little while we were sleeping, but fortunately, I didn't see it. Mina wanted to know what snow is. I tried to explain it, but she didn't really understand. On we rolled and rolled. Would we never get out of that car and stop living in the little houses? Mom said that we got to a house called Niagara Falls. It was so terribly cold in the bedroom. I shivered and shivered. We snuggled a lot. Mina went under the covers.

In the morning, the room was finally warm, but then we were stuffed into our boxes and taken out to the cold car. How much longer? I have resigned myself to the morning ritual of getting into the box. Mina, on the other hand, is getting worse and worse about it. She hid deep under the covers, but Mom and Dad saw her easily as a big lump in the bed, and picked her up. She fought and fought getting into the box, but, of course, they won and in she went. The car stopped a couple of times, but eventually we got somewhere with people who hugged Mom and Dad. We got out of the warm car into the cold, but then we went right into a house. It was a pretty big house with just one problem – there were other felines there! I think I know them. They are called Mr. Purr and Millie! I believe that I knew them in Malden house. I thought I was rid of them forever, but here we are again.

The next morning, we did not get up and go into the boxes. We did not get into the car and roll. We ate breakfast and hid. We found a nice, quiet place in the wall in a bedroom where Richie (Mom's grandson) lived. I remember him from when he stayed with us in the house called Phoenix. We were so scared that we would have to move on again, that we hardly ever came out of the wall for days. Sometimes we didn't even eat. Did I say that?

Well remembering all of this stuff has made me very tired. Nighty night!

Yours,
Apache

Journey into Madness!

I've been playing with some new toys, and someone named Linda has been helping me to play.

Am I still alive? Miss Patchy suggested the title for this page, but I don't really know what it means. She says that a journey is like a trip. Well, what is a trip? Anyway, we had an awful ordeal, Miss Patchy and I. We were put into our boxes every morning and taken to the car to roll away somewhere. It was so scary! Sometimes I tried so hard not to get into the box, but Miss Patchy said that Mom and Dad will always win that fight, and she was absolutely right. I hated all those little houses where we lived for the night. They smelled funny and they were small, and I just wanted to be back home, where I felt safe. I hated rolling in the car, too. Mostly Miss Patchy and I slept when we were in the car, so I don't remember a lot of it.

First, there was all the packing away of familiar things, and the loss of our furniture. Where did it go and why? Now I understand it a little better, since we seem to be at home in a new place. It is much bigger than those little places where we lived for the nights. I feel a little safer now, except for the other felines who also live here. The one named Mr. Purr is very frightening. He says he is the boss here and I need to just stay out of his way and do whatever he says. Miss Patchy says that she knew him a long time ago. She didn't like him then and she doesn't like him now, but she's not really afraid of him. She fights with him, although not so much anymore. She is very brave. I wish I could be like her. One reason I don't like him much is that he yells all the time. Miss Patchy said that he didn't used to yell and that maybe he can't hear too well. That might be right, since sometimes I come right up to him and he doesn't notice until he actually sees me and then he is very startled. Wow! I would hate it if I couldn't hear. Maybe he's not such a bad guy after all.

The other feline is called Millie and I like to intimidate her. Miss Patchy said that's what I do, but I don't really know that word. Anyway, when we meet, I hiss at her and she mostly runs away and I chase her, except for sometimes when she hisses back. It is fun. Sometimes, Millie even comes right in front of me, teasing me. It's a good game.

At first it was very cold in this new house, and Miss Patchy and I spent a lot of time in a wall, refusing to come out, even sometimes we didn't eat. That is very unusual for Miss Patchy, but not so much for me. Finally, things are getting warmer, and the windows are open sometimes. The windows here are much different from home, and there are a lot more of them. They look different, and there are a lot of things to see when I look out, plus they are easier to get to. There are lots of birds to watch. I wish I could get to them, but again, there are screens, and I can't get out. I have to be satisfied just to watch and switch my tail, thinking about what I would do to them if I ever caught them. When I look out the windows, mostly all I see are many brown stick-like things. I'm not sure what they are.

What a terrible ordeal we have gone through. I just can't stop thinking about being in the box for so long and staying in those horrible little houses. Some of them were not so terribly bad, but they just weren't home. Some of them smelled very bad and some were not very good. Some were not too bad, but home is best. Will we ever be home again? Miss Patchy says that we probably won't ever be in Phoenix home again. She has some experience, and thinks that we are probably in our new home now.

I was very frightened the other day. Once again, we were put into the boxes, both of us. We went to the car and rolled away. I thought for sure we would end up in one of those awful little houses for the night, but instead, we went to see the vet. Almost as bad, but at least we went home when we were done there. The vet poked and prodded until I thought I would go crazy. Then she gave me a shot. Miss Patchy got the same. What is happening now? I think we have to go back again later on. Mom and Dad are talking about flying somewhere. Well, we don't have wings, so I don't think we will be flying anywhere any time soon. I talked to Miss Patchy about this, but she says I shouldn't be so sure about things. She says that Mom and Dad have talked about flying here and flying there, and they don't have wings. Hm-m-m-m! We will have to think about this for a while to see if we can figure it out.

Maybe if I play with some toys, I can think better. My mind will be clearer.

Regards,
Mina

What Next?

I have been sleeping and napping a lot. Both Mina and I now spend a lot of time on Mom and Dad's bed. Mr. Purr and Millie almost never come into that room, so we are pretty safe there.

Mr. Purr keeps playing boss, and he and I get into some big fights. Mina is terrified of him, so she just tries to stay out of his way. She tries to boss Millie around, and so do I. Things are beginning to calm down a little now, and sometimes Millie even teases us somewhat, so that we will come after her. Toys are appearing for Mina to play with, and that makes her happy. She also watches the birds from the windows. There are a lot of windows here, and they are easy to get to. Lots of birds and other things to see and hear.

Sometimes I sleep in the tower that we brought from home. It makes me feel a little safe. In the evening, sometimes I will lie on the couch beside Mom or Dad. The others will never bother me there. Ha! Both Mom and Dad are bigger than Mr. Purr, so he won't try to fight with them. I miss home.

Will we ever see home again? I am beginning to think that we will never be there again, but maybe we will have a new home. Are we there now? Probably not. Dad keeps talking about going to live in a turkey. What? Why does turkey play such a large part in our lives? We eat turkey at Thanksgiving, and I suspect that humans come from turkeys, as I have mentioned previously, but now we are all going to live in one? This is very puzzling to me. I have talked to Mina about it, and she is even more confused than I am. Dad talks about flying into the turkey, but none of us has wings.

Also, are there different sized turkeys? The one we eat at Thanksgiving isn't big enough for even just me to get into. Now we are all going to live in one? This is going to take a lot of thought on my part. Mina, too. Will it be cold in this turkey? Will it be hot in this turkey? Can we eat it if we get hungry? Very strange! Life appears to be full of surprises and little lessons to be learned.

In the meantime, we need to survive living with these other felines. Millie is pretty docile and tries to stay out of our way. Mina insists on going after Millie, and then Mom has to yell at her. I guess Mina just wants to be the boss of somebody. I keep telling her to just forget about it and get along, but she doesn't listen very well. Breakfast and supper are getting easier. They give Mr. Purr some of the wet food and move his dish a little way from ours, and Mina's is moved away, too. Millie usually doesn't partake of meals with the rest of us, preferring to just snack throughout the day, or when no one else is there. She misses out on the wet food most of the time, but I don't think she really minds very much. If she is there when it is served, then she gets some. If not, she doesn't get any.

Mom has not been making food for us for a long time. That's another thing that makes me think we are not yet in our new home. I miss that food. It was very delicious! Maybe someday she will make it again, and we will all be happy together again. In a turkey??? Lots to think about!

I guess I will take a nap now so that I can think. I do my best thinking while I am napping.

Yours,
Apache

Life Goes on

Well, I took a nice, long nap on Mom and Dad's bed and am feeling ready to go. Where? Where can one go except downstairs or upstairs?

Mr. Purr and I have a truce. I wouldn't say we actually get along, but we don't get into big fights anymore. We hiss and growl at each other sometimes, but no "knock down drag out fights," as Mom would put it. A sort of peace has descended upon this house. There is just one wrong note here. Dad has disappeared. He and Mom got in the car and rolled away. Dad had some suitcases, so I suspect that he will be back some time before too long. Mom came back by herself and seemed sad, but I'm not sure why. I do miss Dad though. Mom says that we will go to see Dad soon and be with him. That does not sound like a good idea, because going somewhere means going into the box again.

It is a lot warmer than it was when we first came to this house. It's great having the windows open so that we can smell the outdoors and hear the birds. Linda says that one window is called "Cat TV," because we can see where the birds come to eat and drink. What fun! Also, we can get on the table in the front room and look out another window to see pretty much the same things. This is not a bad house! Mina likes it here, because Linda plays with her a lot. Mr. Purr and Millie are pretty old, and they don't play too much anymore, so Linda likes to watch the little fool, I mean Mina, jump in the air trying to catch Ribbon. Ribbon is a new member of our family. Linda gave it to Mina, who loves it a lot. It is sort of fun to watch her leap into the air.

Mom is busy doing something on the eating room table. There are her computer, a funny kind of box and lots of what she calls records or albums. Quite often, she sits at the table and puts one of the records in the box, turns it on and has things on over her head and on her ears. I don't hear anything or see anything. Why does she waste her time with a box that doesn't do anything? Oh well, whoever said that humans could be understood? They do strange things all the time. I mean, really, why would anyone want to stand in a little room and get wet? Ugh! It makes me shudder just to think about it. Mom took me in with her once, because I had some pee on me in places I couldn't reach. Suffice it to say that a trip to the vet caused it to be on me. She made me come out of the box and then she turned on the water. Oh, how awful it was! At least she was also getting wet, even though she didn't seem to mind at all. Once we were thoroughly wet, she shut off the water and tried to wrap me in a towel. I didn't like that very much, and escaped from the bathroom as soon as I could. She does that every morning, no matter what house we are in!

Mina says she wants to go outside and get a bird. I told her that she can only think about it, because they will never let us go outside. Mr. Purr and Millie are sometimes allowed to go out, but they are old and slow and usually come in when Linda tells them to. One time, though, Millie hid, and Linda was a little upset with her. Finally, she came in and all was peaceful again.

Mom has been taking things out of boxes and putting them in different boxes and putting them in the back room.

When Mom and Dad went away one day, with two cars, a lot of boxes disappeared from the house. I don't know what they did with them, but they are completely gone and, I think, not coming back. One of the cars did not come back, either. We used to look out the window and see the big white car sitting in the driveway, but it is no longer there. Mom is very busy, though. She goes places and comes back, sometimes with stuff, sometimes not. Sometimes she says she has been "downtown," wherever that is. She says it costs her a lot of money to go there, so I don't know why she goes. There is something called an "apple still" that she has to see and then she goes to a turkey thing. I don't know what it is, but it starts with "con."

Besides being busy, Mom is a little stressed – actually a lot stressed. Sometimes she goes places with Linda and/or Richie, but so far she always comes back. I'm afraid that one day she won't come back. What will we do then? We can't stay here. Millie is so upset about our being here, that she sometimes leaves puddles and little presents for Linda. She says she doesn't like our being here, and she is protesting. Of course, with Mina being here and trying to boss her around, she feels that she has no status, because she says we all pick on her. I don't think that's true. We don't pick on her all the time, just a lot of the time. She's easy to pick on, except sometimes she does growl and hiss back at us. I think that if we stay here much longer, she will try to get revenge on us.

Mom keeps saying that soon we will fly away to be with Dad. With what wings? Are we birds? I must take a nap and keep on thinking about this. It's very puzzling.

Yours,
Apache

Now What?

I've just had a restorative nap and did I ever need it!

We went to the vet again today and not only did we get another shot, but he put something in our necks. It was really big! They were all talking about a "chip." Mom says that we now have a chip in our necks so that we can never get lost. I'm not sure how that could work, but if that's what Mom wants to believe, I guess I can go along with that. I sure don't want to be lost!

Mom is getting more and more frantic! Things are not always working right with the funny box on the table or the things on her ears. Sometimes she says she can't hear anything through those things. Is that what she was doing? Listening to something? Does the box make noise? Sometimes she says the box is not working right. I never saw it do anything, so I have no comment on it. A while ago, we had a yard sale, and soon we will have another one. How dull and boring! We never get to go out and help. We just stay inside and watch all the people, although most of the time I would rather just nap on Mom's bed. Since Dad is gone, it is just Mom's bed now. He has been gone a long time now, but Mom still says that we will fly away to be with him. I'm beginning to doubt her sanity.

Mom has made more trips to that "downtown" place and she still complains about the cost. Just don't go there! That would cost her nothing at all. She complains all the time about money. She says she still has to pay bills, and that she will be lucky to have enough money for our trip. That does not sound good – the "trip" part. I think that means box time. She still keeps talking about living in a turkey and flying. I'm pretty sure now that she is going crazy. That "living in a turkey" thing just doesn't sound right. At least she still feeds us well and tries to keep peace between the four of us. I hope Mr. Purr and Millie are not going to live in the turkey, too. That would be just too much!

A man comes over sometimes, bringing stuff to put in the back room. Mom says he is her X. Linda calls him Dad. Is he an X or a Dad? Humans have such strange things in their lives! Anyway, he never touches us, and we don't stick around to see what he wants, so I guess he is pretty harmless. One time, he came when nobody was home, except the four of us. He has a key so he could come in and put stuff in the back room.

One day, Mom went to see what she said was a "cheesy movie." I like cheese, why didn't she take me? Richie went to work, and Linda was off somewhere, I think a dinner. Is that the same as supper? Mom used to have dinners. A lot of people would come over and she sometimes had to set up an extra table. She would cover the tables with cloths and put the good china and silver out. She would cook a lot and then people would come and bring more food. They all sat around and ate, and talked a lot. Mom usually had music on and after a while, the people would leave. Cherokee and I would usually get some good food out of it.

Mom spends a lot of time on her computer, too. She says she is ordering things to take to the turkey. Boy, am I getting tired of hearing about this turkey. It must be pretty big and important for us to be able to live in it and give it presents. I wish people would just shut up about it, because it makes me uneasy. I don't like to travel, and I'm sure that this involves traveling.

I think I need to take a very long nap to try to work it out.

Yours,
Apache

Will it Ever End?

Thank heavens for restorative naps!

We went to the vet again. No shots this time. They looked in our ears, rubbed some stuff on the back of our necks, and made us eat something. How awful! I tried so hard to get away, but nothing worked. They got the towel again, so I couldn't really use my feet and legs. Mina usually doesn't struggle much and lets Mom hold her for those nasty people. Mom got some papers and then we came home. This afternoon, she had to go see USDA. What a strange name! She got some papers there, too. She says it is for our trip. She says now that we are flying to brussels. Is that a food, also? I've heard of brussels sprouts. Mom says they are delicious. What's going on here anyway? Dad is going to pick us up at the airport in brussels sprouts. I think I'm very confused. Mina, too, but she just goes along with everything, as long as she can play with Ribbon. It is her favorite toy.

Mom has been packing all her clothes in suitcases. She says that she can't fit everything into the smaller one she has. Linda brought her a big one, but not everything fits in that one either, so she is packing both of them. This is looking very serious. She has been packing stuff for us, too. I think I'm getting a little scared. The last time she packed, we spent many days in the car and slept in the little houses at night. Will this be like that? She still talks about flying. I think she is seriously deluded, but what can I say or do? Mina just plays with Ribbon and doesn't worry about anything else. Silly thing!

Life goes on here. Linda works in her garden – she is growing vegetables! Why not something useful, like meat? I heard Mom say that meat grows – why not have a meat garden? I think I would be tempted to help in that kind of garden. Linda has planted peppers, tomatoes, even potatoes. What a useless waste of time. Mom says she wishes she could be here when things get ripe, but she will be in the turkey by that time. So strange! It's as though she really wants to live in a turkey. It's as though she really believes it. I guess we'll see I'm afraid!

Not too much else has happened around here. That's probably a good thing, since most of the things that have happened have not been good, at least from my viewpoint. Books have come in the mail, and Mom has packed them. She says she will need them to read in the turkey. Turkey, turkey, turkey! I'm getting really sick of hearing about it. What kind of human would want to live in a turkey?

Well, I seriously need a nap now, because things are getting very worrisome and I would rather just not think about this stuff. Hopefully, I will have some good dreams.

Yours,
Apache

Oh, No!!

At least I have had a nice nap!

Well, it was as I suspected, we were unceremoniously put into our boxes and put in the car. Off we rolled and got out in a very big, very noisy place. We went inside where there were way too many humans, making way too much noise. Mom talked to someone and gave her the two suitcases she has been packing and then we had to go somewhere else, to a quiet place. We waited in a narrow hallway for a while, then someone came with a flat stick (Mom called it a scanner), and Mom had to take each of us out of our boxes and hold us tight while a man put the stick inside our boxes, then by us. We were both glad to go back inside the boxes, as they were not nearly as scary as the hallway and the man with the stick.

After that, Mom said goodbye to us and walked away! We were terrified! Where was Mom going? We were with strangers! Later on, someone came and took us in our boxes outside, then into a little room. Mom was nowhere around. Mina was a little panicky. A little while later, the little room began to vibrate and there was a lot of noise. The room continued to vibrate and, since I was very sleepy, I went to sleep. I think Mina did, too. We woke up when someone picked up our boxes, took us outside again, and put us into another small room. This one also vibrated and made a lot of noise.

Finally, after sleeping for a while, the vibrating stopped and someone came and took our boxes outside again and then into another big, noisy place. Our boxes were on a rolling thing. All of a sudden, there was Mom. She appeared to be very happy to see us, almost as happy as we were to see her. We had thought we would never see her again. She told us that we were in brussels (brussels sprouts?). I don't know where or what it is, and I sure don't know how we got there. Anyway, before long, there was Dad. We hadn't seen him for a long time, and it was nice to see him again. All the suitcases were piled on the rolling thing with us and we rolled outside, to where Dad's car was. We were packed into the car with a whole lot of other stuff. Mom said we had flown here. What delusions! I still don't have any wings.

After rolling for a while, the car stopped and we all got out and went into one of those little houses again. Mom put down the litter box, although we didn't know that's what it was at first, because it smelled funny. Dad put some dirt in it, but we still weren't sure, so Mom peed in it a little, and then we knew. What a relief! We had some food to eat, and water to drink. Not much like home, but it was not bad.

In the morning, everything was packed up and off we rolled once again. We stopped several times, but kept right on rolling through the night and all the next day. Mom and Dad ate, but we didn't! Not that we were all that hungry. All that rolling just makes us sleepy. We continued to roll through the next night. Mom said something about "beljum, luxburg, frans, switz, itali". We stopped at a place and waited for a while, then the car drove onto what Mom calls a boat. They called it a fairy, although I never saw a fairy or any other magical creature. I think they were lying to us. We went upstairs on the boat and there were lots of people, none of whom seemed to know how to talk. It was just gibberish coming out of their mouths, although I could tell that a lot of them liked us. After dark, we went to a really tiny house. Mom and Dad slept on tiny, little beds and we just explored the tiny bathroom and that was pretty much it. At least we had food, water, and litter box.

In the morning, we got into the car again and rolled off. Where to? Who knows? Mom said there were lots of trees and said something about "grease." We could not see the trees or the grease, since we were pretty well packed in. They finally let us out of the boxes, so we could move around and see stuff, but it was a little scary. Things were moving by the car so fast! We sat with Mom for a little while, but it was better just to find a comfortable place and go to sleep. When the daylight was gone and it had been dark for a while, we stopped again. We stayed there for some time, while Dad went into places and handled a lot of papers. Then we went to another place to stop and were there even longer, with more papers. Finally we were able to roll again, and we found another little house to sleep in. Mom says we are in the turkey now. Somehow it's just not what I expected. I thought there would be a lot of meat and bones. Maybe Mom is just kidding me. This just doesn't look like something to eat, since there are trees and houses and stuff in it.

The morning brought more packing up and we rolled off again. Before too long, we came to a place where we parked. Mom and Dad went off somewhere and left us in the car. They came back a long time later (long after dark), opened the back of the car, and showed us to some people. Finally they got in the car and we rolled off again. Fortunately, it was not too long before we stopped at a little house again. Those stops are usually nice, though small. Dad did not stay in the little house with us.

In the morning, we rolled off again, and then Mom and we stayed at another little house, while Dad went somewhere else. It was all a little confusing to us, but bearable. After all that, we rolled away again in the morning, but just a little way. We went to an actual house, where we were put into a room with our litter box and some food and water. The door was shut and we were alone. We looked around a little, but then slept. Mom and Dad came back later, but then things were packed up once more and off we went, rolling down the road at night. All the other stuff was out of the car, just a few suitcases and us, plus four humans.

When we stopped (after a long nap), the air smelled different. We went into a place they called an apartment. It had two rooms and a bathroom, with some outdoor places with screens on them. Sort of like the patio at home, but up off the ground. It was nice there, even though Mom and Dad, Dad's brother, and Dad's mother came and went a lot. One day, Mom slept most of the day, because she was so tired from all the rolling we had done. She was tired?!!!! What about us? The next day, they went somewhere together and came back smelling different again. In fact, they were wet and it smelled like funny-type water. Mom said they were at the beach and that we were in a place called "Alanya." What's a beach? What's Alanya? After two days there, we went back to the house and our room. Mom slept in the next room, and she opened the door between us so we could have a little more room.

All of these memories are making me very tired, so I must go and take a nap.

Yours,
Apache

Constant Fear

I have played a little bit, but I'm not really feeling up to it much lately.

We have come to a place where we seem to be staying for a while. It is nice not to be in the box anymore, but it's kind of a scary place. We are kept mainly in two rooms, with some air coming through and some windows to look out of. However, there's not much to see, mostly a wall.

Last night, the windows in the room where Mom sleeps were open and had screens on them. Before, just a window on top was open, and we couldn't get to it. The bottom windows' being open was very nice, as we could hear a lot more things. That was not always a good thing, though. Some time after dark, a loud man's voice came in the window. He was sort of singing, and it was scary. Both Miss Patchy and I were scared, but Mom wasn't. Maybe the man's voice is not so bad, but if I hear it again, I think I will still be afraid. Mom says we shouldn't worry about it, because the man, who she says is called a "muzin" is calling everyone to pray so we should be happy to hear it. I'll have to think about that. I'm not sure what praying is, but the way Mom says it, I think it isn't a bad thing.

Miss Patchy and I mostly stay in Mom's closet, because we feel safe there. In the last few days, Mom has let us come out of the two rooms, and there is a food room, and couch room where people sit and sleep. There are also some bathrooms, although one of them seems strange to me. It smells like a toilet, but it doesn't look like a toilet. It looks like a hole in the floor, and there is a water place there, too.

When we are out of the two rooms, sometimes a strange person comes out. Mom says it is Dad's mother. She scares me, though. The hair on her head has all kinds of colors on it that are sometimes pretty, and she ties it under her chin. Every day it is different. I have never seen hair like that before. She always has glasses on, unlike Mom and Dad, who just wear them sometimes. Her clothes come to the floor, so I'm not sure that she has legs, or what. Also, her voice is scratchy and loud. Sometimes in the morning, I have heard her head whistle and squeak. Mom says that it is her hearing aid we hear whistling. I don't know what that is. She is very frightening to me. When she gets up, Miss Patchy and I go to the closet and stay there.

Mom found the other litter box yesterday – the one she calls portable. She couldn't find it before, so we were using part of my box. Now it will smell all the time. I hope I don't ever have to get in it again, because I hate it, and the smell will make it worse.

Mom says that this is our new home. I don't know if I like it. Maybe if I can get to know the rest of the place it will be better. It smells funny, though, and neither Miss Patchy nor I like the smell. It's very strong! Mom says it is mothballs that we smell. Ugh! There are a lot of other unfamiliar smells, too. I need to investigate them in order to know what they are all about.

Dad cooked us some food, but I still just prefer the dry food. It smells nice, but I just don't like it. Miss Patchy has trouble eating the dry food, because she doesn't have a lot of teeth left, so she needs to eat the wet food. I think that's funny! I have all of my teeth! Does that make me better than Miss Patchy? I think so.

I miss home very much, but I think it is gone and we are now here, and will never see home again. Mom says that we flew. I don't believe it. I think we came in a great big car. Miss Patchy and I were in our boxes in a little room, and it vibrated a lot, but we still did not have any wings, so how could we have been flying? Birds fly, and bugs fly, but felines do not fly, neither do humans. Silly Mom!

Mom says that we are now living in the turkey that she and Dad have been talking about for a long time. That's another silly thing she has said. It doesn't smell like a turkey, and I don't see any meat. How could we be in a turkey? Mom is strange sometimes, but I love her anyway. I love to lie on her chest and put my paws around her neck. Then I purr a lot and she pets me. It is a wonderful time.

Well, I need to think about playing. Ribbon has come here, too, and so has Mousey, so not everything is strange. Mom also brought the furry beds. It's too warm for them now, but maybe it will be cold here, too. It's time to think about playing.

Regards,
Mina

Are Things Getting Better?

Naps are my life right now. That's about all we can do, since we are stuck in two rooms.

I must say, though, that things are getting better. Even though we have just two rooms, the food is good – Dad cooked it, and the closet is comfortable. Mom complains about fur on the suitcases, but why is that a problem? Anyway, both Mina and I are feeling better about everything. Even the litter is good. It does not smell at all like the stuff we had at home. It doesn't smell at all, so I never feel bad about stepping in it. There are no lumps or anything to get in the way.

I have been feeling a lot better recently. My legs do not hurt so much. Mom says she is putting something in my food to help. I guess it is working. She put stuff in the food at home, but it did not work as well. Dad said he paid a lot for it, so he is very glad that it is working so well.

There are other felines around. We can smell them and sometimes hear them outside the windows. A little while ago, Mina and I were allowed out of our rooms, and we explored. Mom said we could go outside in the garden, but we didn't feel very secure about that. It was a hot day, so I went down into the basement. It was very dark and cool there, and I could smell the other felines, but they weren't there when I went down. I stayed down for a while, and Mom was really mad when I came up. She said I was very, very dirty and she made me take a shower. Oh, how I hated that. After the shower, she said I was still very dirty. I don't like her saying that. I take great pride in my appearance. She still says it, but also says that I am getting cleaner.

Mina was gone all day and into the darkness. Mom and Dad were calling for her all over. They were afraid that she had panicked and run far away and was unable to find her way back. Personally, I think it would be good riddance! Anyway, they all were sitting at the table out front, on what Mom calls the front porch when evidently Mina showed her face. Instead of the basement, she had spent all day in the attic. It was dirty up there, too, but she didn't have to take a shower. Mom said she was dirty, but not as bad as I was. I'll bet! The little sneak! Because of the basement and the attic, we are no longer allowed out of our rooms, and we really don't want to go out. Too much happens then.

Mom tried to take me outside one day, but I got away and went up to the attic and got dusty. She chased me out and down the stairs. After that, the door was accidently left open, and Mina ran up to the attic. Dad was angry, but he got her down pretty soon. At least it's quiet in our rooms and nothing bad happens. We also haven't been in the car for a long time, so that's a good thing.

Mina is feeling a lot better now. She is eating more (actually, quite a lot), and she has been playing at night. Last night, I did a little playing and explored up in the cupboard in Mom's room. She heard me jiggle the glass things and woke up. She was blaming Mina until she turned on the light and saw that it was me. I'm so glad I feel better. It's very possible that now I can do stuff and Mina will be blamed. That sounds like fun!

One thing that we don't like here is the vacuum cleaner. I thought the one at home was bad, but this one is very big and very loud. I hate it when Mom or Dad use it. Mom says we keep getting fur and stuff on the rugs. That's it, blame us! She gets stuff on the rug, too. We aren't the only ones.

Today, I threw up on one of the rugs. Just a little bit on the rug and a lot on the cardboard under our food dishes. Dad cleaned it up. He is very nice and does a lot of things for Mom, and she really appreciates it.

Well, it's still daylight, time for another nap. I wouldn't want to waste the daylight. I also must get ready for the night!

Yours,
Apache

What Have We Done Wrong?

Mina

I have played quite a bit lately, as I am getting used to this place. There's not much room to play, but every now and then I can jump over Miss Patchy and sometimes somebody will help me to play with Ribbon.

Well, we are in prison. No matter how you look at it, we are in prison. That's Miss Patchy's conclusion, and I believe her. Every time someone comes into the room or leaves the room, we are pushed aside, or told "No!," and the human quickly goes out and shuts the door on us. I'm not sure why we are in prison, but it's not a lot of fun. There are no bars like you see on TV, but we are in prison, just the same. I so much want to explore the rest of this house, and I did a little bit the day I hid in the attic, but since that day, we are not allowed out of our cell, I mean our rooms. At least we have good food and water, litter box, and Mom to snuggle with at night and sometimes during the day, but it is still prison. At least at home we could go out on the patio and watch the buzz birds and bugs, and smell the fresh air, and feel the sunshine on our bodies. I always rolled on the cement as soon as I could get out the door. Mom would always get a little mad, because she said I got dust all over my fur. Who cares about a little dust? Well, I guess Mom does.

What I need is some place to run. I'm afraid my legs will get stiff or something if I don't get to have a good run pretty soon. Mom says that soon we will have plenty of room to run, but I have my doubts about that. She keeps promising. I think we will be stuck here for the rest of our lives. We do have windows, but most of them just show us a wall. One window shows us the back wall, a little place with some holes that are covered up (Mom says it's called a "tandir") with a little roof over it, some dead grass beyond the wall, and some other houses. There are some birds flying around sometimes, and once in a while we can see a human. We also hear some funny bird sounds. Mom says they are roosters crowing, and hens cackling. You could not prove it by me, because I don't know what those are. Mom says that they are chickens. (Why not just say chickens?) That makes Miss Patchy happy, because she loves chicken. I don't know what she would do with a noisy one, though. If it is alive, wouldn't it fight with Miss Patchy? If you can live in a turkey, can you live in a chicken? How big are they?

It would be nice, but very scary, to go outside. There are a lot of strange humans, and we have heard other felines out there. Sometimes the other felines have been in the house, because we have smelled them, especially in the basement and the attic. I'm not sure why I like the attic so much, but it is warm and comforting somehow.

Another thing about this prison is that Mom's computer is always here, so we have easy access to it when she's not around. Miss Patchy has learned how to get on the internet with Dad's phone. It isn't always around, so we can't go online all the time, but we can have fun playing games and writing stuff to publish online later. Mom keeps the dirty clothes in here, too, as well as the detergent she uses to wash them. After she washes the clothes, they smell like the outdoors. Is the dryer outside? There are a lot of things that Miss Patchy and I do not understand about this house, besides why we are kept in prison, but I guess it could be worse. It is clean and dry and has lots of things from home. I will try to like it here.

I hear Mousey calling me to play, so I'd better go. Miss Patchy is already asleep, since she got rid of a big hairball this morning, and her stomach was hurting her. She's better now, but she needs her nap.

Regards,
Mina

Whose Voice is it?

Well, I have been getting a lot of naps lately, as there is not much to do in two rooms. I still don't know why we are imprisoned.

Anyway, that muzin person has been calling out a lot lately. Mom says it is because it is "Ramazan," whatever that is. She is not getting much sleep, except for naps during the day, with me. She always wakes up when Dad and "Memmet" get up to eat in the early, early morning, while it is still dark. I know they are eating, because I can smell the food. They never invite Mina or me, though. That seems a little cruel, but what can I do? Mom can never get back to sleep, and she blames us. Just because we like to play and fight, and then I get hungry.

To get back to the muzin! His voice is very loud and echoey. It just comes out of the sky and is a little scary, since we can't see anyone. Mom and Dad talk sometimes about a person called "God." Is this another relative? They say he lives in heaven, in the sky. Since the voice is coming out of the sky, is it possibly this God who is calling out? They say he is watching us all the time, and knows if we are bad or good (is that like Santa?). I personally can't see how anyone can live in the sky, as there are no houses up there that I can see. Sometimes I see clouds, and sometimes there are bright flashes in the sky, but no houses. Does he live in a cloud? Actually, what is a cloud made of? Just because it doesn't look like a house, maybe it is made of something else that he can live in. Mom always says that not all houses look alike. She says that there are some that you can see right through, so maybe God's house is like that, and I just keep missing him when I look up. Of course, here I really can't see too much of the sky, unless I get up in the back window. There I can see a lot, but with the pain in my legs, I can't always get up there. I will have to ponder this some more.

Mom has been brushing the rugs every morning. She says she doesn't want to leave too much fur for Dad's mother to complain about. She does not like us at all and is always waving a piece of cloth at us, and yelling at Mom or Dad. Mom really wants to get out of this prison as soon as possible to get away from her. Dad gets all nervous before he comes to see us, because of Dad's mother's yelling. She yells so much, I keep wondering why she still has a voice.

I guess I will go to sleep for a nice, long nap and think about it long and hard.

Yours,
Apache

Why Are We Still in Prison?

I can't find Mousey anywhere. Mom says that he was totally bald, but he was still fun to play with. He is probably just hiding somewhere. I'll have to look around some more. At least Ribbon is still here and full of fun.

Mom says that soon we will be in a better place to live and will have plenty of room to run and play. That's good, but she keeps saying that, and it keeps being a lot longer than soon.

I have found a new place to hide when Mom and Dad are gone. Dad's mother keeps coming into the room when they are gone and she keeps waving a cloth at me. I am very scared of her, since she doesn't know how to talk, she just makes noises with her mouth. Dad seems to know what those noises mean, though, and he can make those same noises. Anyway, I have found a way to get up under not just the blanket, but under the memory foam mattress, too. The first time I hid there, Mom came in and couldn't find me. She called and called, and Dad was afraid that his mother had let me get out, but Mom finally found me. I don't know how she does that. How can she know that I am under the covers or the mattress? It's a puzzle to me. I know she can't see me, and I can't see her. I'll have to think a lot about that.

I have been going "stir crazy," at least that's what Mom calls it. I just can't get up much speed running in two rooms. I hope there will be more rooms in the new place, if we ever get there. I'm beginning to think that it doesn't actually exist and that Mom is just making it up to make us feel better. That would be cruel, I think.

I saw one of the outside felines the other day. How lucky they are to be able to run around anywhere they want, with no one to put them in prison or tell them stories of another place that probably doesn't even exist. If she wasn't so good to us, I think I would seriously try to get out and join the outside felines. They are all small, so I don't think I would have a problem with them.

I have learned how the doors open. There are handles that I can grab hold of. I tried to open the door a few nights ago, but Mom put a box in front of the door. Mom told Dad that she doesn't think I am heavy enough to actually pull all the way down on the handle, because it is quite stiff. Maybe I need to eat more! Mom says she doesn't want me to get out because there is mouse poison around. What is poison? Evidently it is not a good thing, so why is it all around? Also, Mom says that Dad's mother would have a fit because of my fur getting on stuff.

A stranger came to visit the other day and, even though Dad's mother doesn't like us, she brought the visitor in to see us. The visitor seemed nice, and Memmet was here, too. I think I like him, as he is a lot like Dad. I have allowed him to pet me a little bit. Mom said that the visitor is Dad's sister. So, we have a brother, a sister, and a mother. Are there more yet? Too many people! Miss Patchy does not seem to mind so much anymore if anyone comes into the room. She is really getting old and forgetting how things should be.

Well, I have to take a nap now so I will be up for some good playing later.

Regards,
Mina

A New Place

I can't seem to nap very well, but I did sleep last night. I'm tired though, and a little scared.

Well, it actually does exist! We came to the new place to live yesterday. I'm still a little afraid of it and its strange noises and lots of human voices, but Mom says I will get used to it. Dad's mother comes here during the day, and I don't like that, but at least we can get away from her and hide. Mom fed us before she left, and left us here alone, but she was here for quite a while after she fed us and then I was very hungry. They came this morning, but it was pretty late, and I was half starved. Mina always has her dry food in the dish, so she almost never gets hungry.

Mom and Dad found us in the basement this morning. It is cooler down there, but they were upset because our paws were so dirty. Why all this concern over dirty paws? I will get them clean. Why isn't the basement clean, anyway? I don't get it. My paws would stay very clean if the basement was clean. However, they say they don't want us in the basement. I don't know why. It's a very interesting place. There are lots of things down there that smell very familiar, lots of boxes with stuff in them. They smell like Mom, so I like it there. Mom comes down to the basement and does stuff with the things in the boxes. I like it that she is there, as it is very comforting.

Besides Mom, Dad, and Dad's mother, there is another person here. I think Mom and Dad said that he is Dad's nephew. He seems okay, but I'm just not sure yet. Mom gets upset because I hiss at her, but all this is just so new and frightening. Mom says that she is going to fly back home and that later on Dad, Mina, and I will fly back home. There is that silly delusion about flying! We still have no wings! Very strange ideas that humans get into their heads!

Dad took me upstairs to eat breakfast, but I didn't feel all that hungry. I ate a little and then went back to the basement. I saw Dad's mother on the way down, and I almost turned around to go back up. However, she just stayed on the couch and didn't wave any cloth at me, so I eventually continued on down to the basement. There is a door to go outside on the way down, but I don't think I want to go out. We heard dogs last night, and I think they are always right outside the door.

We found the litter box. Of course, yesterday Mom let us out of the box right by it, so it wasn't too hard to find. It's good to have all the comforts of home; I just wish we were really home. Mom says we will go home – I can hardly wait! Where we are living now is called Office. That seems odd to me, because in the house called Phoenix, we had a room called Office. Mom kept her computer and stuff in that room. There is a computer here, but other rooms, too. It's confusing. In one room, there is a big couch and a closet thing, but not much else other than bags and boxes. When we go upstairs from there, there is a sort of bathroom. Mina says that she thinks she could use that instead of going down to the litter box, but I don't know. There is a big hole in the floor and I could slip. Lots of water in that room, too. The room where I hide is sort of like part of a food room. There is what looks like a counter top, a funny round sink, and some cabinets. Then there is another room where there is a refrigerator and some more cabinets. There are some windows in that room, but they are up high. Mina will be able to get up there, but I don't think I will be able to. There is also a big window in the couch room. That one I can see out of. The door downstairs from there was covered from the outside, so we couldn't see out at all. This is a pretty strange place.

In the big couch room, there is something that looks like a chair lying on its back. I'm not sure why it would be like that. It's much easier to sit on when it is standing up. I don't think that Mina and I can set it up, so we will have to wait and see if Dad or Mom will do it. I think it would be nice to lie on.

Well, Mina is back behind the cabinets in the part-food room. She can get out on her own, so no one is worried about her. I'm sure I couldn't even get down into that space, let alone get out, so I'm not even going to try. Lying in the cabinet is good enough for me.

I think it is time to take a nap. I got tired eating and coming back down to the basement, so I need this nap.

Yours,
Apache

Back Again

   I haven't felt much like playing lately. We spent a couple of days at the new place to live, but we didn't like it at all. I found a cozy place in the half food room, right behind the cabinets. It was a little hard to get out of, but it was worth it. No one could get to me there, or so I thought.

   We didn't like the place because it smelled bad and had some gritty dust all over it. The dust is what was smelling bad. There were lots of dogs around outside last night, and we didn't like that either. All the windows were closed, too. It was awfully lonely without Mom and Dad. We've stayed alone before, but in our own home, so it wasn't so terribly bad. We still had familiar things around us for comfort. Miss Patchy says she thinks that they don't love us anymore. I'm not so sure, but she could be right.

   Before they left to go home the second day, Dad got me out from behind the cabinet and put me in the box with Miss Patchy. We were both pretty mad about that, and then riding in that car again. The car stopped a couple of times and we thought that we were going to have a long trip again, like before. However, the last time we stopped, we all got out and they took us back into the house again. We're not crazy to be back where Dad's mother is, but it's better than that awful new place to live. They apologized to us and said we could stay at the house. We will have to watch Dad's mother, though; she is sneaky and always leaves the door open. Sometimes I think she wants us to go outside, but I've been out there and it's not all that great. It was fun to chase the feline Mom calls

Little Bit, but it's a little scary out there, too. There are lots of dogs barking all the time, especially at night.

We kept seeing Little Bit from our windows. She is small and lives with the other felines. Sometimes she has been in the house, because we smell her. One day, we were out of our two rooms and in the couch room. I jumped up to look out the window. There was no screen and the window was open. As I was sitting there, I saw Little Bit on the ground below the window. Immediately I jumped to the ground. She began to run and I was right behind her. We ran very fast, which felt very good to me. Little Bit turned the corner of the house and then ran around to the back. She disappeared, but I sniffed a little and saw that she had gone into the basement. I went right after her, but could not find her at all. I then went back into the house. That fast run was very invigorating and I slept well that night.

I would like to check out the food room, but when I am allowed out for a few minutes, the food room door is always closed. I know it's the food room, because I can smell food in there. Miss Patchy doesn't seem to care a lot, because she sleeps most of the time. When we do go out of our rooms, most of the other doors are closed to us, so we really can't explore at all. I'm so bored in those two rooms. I know every little tiny place and everything that is in them. I have looked out the back window and the side window uncountable times. There's really nothing much to see out the side window, except for a wall and, occasionally, Little Bit or one of her friends as they walk through there. Where will Little Bit live in the cold weather? Mom says it will get very cold here. Then I will be glad to be in these two rooms instead of outdoors with the outside felines.

Well, I'm getting sleepy from boredom, and there's nothing much to play with. I can't find ribbon, and Mom says that Dad's mother doesn't like my squeaky mice because they scare her. She thinks they're real when she first sees them. She doesn't like mice, I guess. That's too bad, because Miss Patchy says they taste pretty good. Oh well, I guess there's no accounting for tastes.

I will take a nap and try to find something to play with later. If I take a nice, long nap now, I can be awake when Mom is sleeping and maybe I can get her to play with me then.

Regards,
Mina

What Now?

I've just had a much-needed nap. Things have been hectic and I get so tired.

Mom has been packing, packing, and repacking. Now she says that she will fly home by herself and Dad will bring us later. Plans keep changing over and over again. She says she has her ticket and will be going home on September 11. I don't know when that is, but it must be soon. She says she doesn't want to leave us here, so why will she? Why doesn't she just stay, too? We don't want her to go. It's not that we don't love Dad, because we love him a lot, we just need both of them here with us.

Now there has been another change. Dad got a call the other day and said that someone wanted to give Mom a job. There is that job thing again. At least they don't want to give me a job! She and Dad went away early one day and came back at night. They seemed pretty happy, now they say that Mom will not be flying away. Well, that's okay with me, but I'm not sure what has happened to change things. We are still here in these two rooms, both Mom and us, and everything seems to be the same.

On another day, Mom packed up her two big suitcases and she and Dad left the house. They were gone several days, but only Dad came back. Where is Mom? Has she actually flown away? Mina and I are very concerned. Mom has escaped from prison, but we are still here. It's true that we have Dad, and sometimes he sleeps on the bed where Mom slept. In fact, sometimes he lets us come out of our rooms and sleep with him in the couch room. Dad's mother sleeps there on the couch. I know that her knees hurt her a lot, so I decided to go and lie on them to keep them warm for her, but she didn't like it very much. Sometimes humans just have no sense at all. Anyway, we can go into the couch room at night, so that's some improvement over our two rooms. Why couldn't we have done that sooner, when Mom was still here? Life is just a big mystery sometimes. We do not see Mom at all, so maybe she has left us for good and we will never see her again. That would be horrible!

I miss Mom so much! Where can she be? I'm sure she wouldn't just leave us, but what else can I think. Dad is gone most of every day, and his mother goes with him, so we are all alone in our two prison rooms. I think I will go crazy. There have just been way too many changes in our lives, and too many people coming and going, and Mom going away a lot. What if we never see her again? Mom, Mom, wherever you are, please come home to your babies! We love you and miss you. Please come back! Dad says that we will be with her soon in our new home. Right! Where have we heard that one before? A new home! Sure! Maybe Mom is dead!

I have to sleep now. If I keep thinking of these things I will go over the edge!

Yours,
Apache

New Beginnings

Well, I've had a good, warm nap. It's so nice to have a comfortable bed with warm covers.

It happened one night. Dad bundled Mina and me into the box and packed all of our stuff in a big car with lots of seats and all those boxes that smell like Mom. The ones that were in the basement at Office. Mina has been so terrified and depressed since Mom left that she can't even talk to me. Anyway, there we were in the box in the big car and we began to roll. Memmet was driving (Mom says he is a better driver than Dad) and Mina and I fell asleep. When we woke up, we heard Mom's voice! Hallelujah! She's not dead after all. She got into the big car with us and told Memmet where to drive. Pretty soon, we were stopped on a street. Mom and Dad tried to unlock a door, but their keys didn't work. They tried to wake someone up, but that didn't work, either. Mom left, and the rest of us stayed behind. Dad and Memmet took all the boxes and things (including us) out of the big car and he drove away. Dad and we spent the night on the sidewalk with our boxes. When it got light, the door opened and someone who lives on the street helped Dad to get the boxes and things up some stairs. Mom came later and was so glad to see us, almost as glad as we were to see her. When everything was up the stairs, Mom and Dad let us out of the box and there we were in a place with several rooms. We were scared, but there really wasn't any place to hide. There wasn't any furniture or anything, except for a very hard, wooden bed. There was a refrigerator and a washer, but no furniture. There wasn't even a closet to hide in.

Our furry beds were there, so we napped, while Mom and Dad left. We were lonely and scared, but at least we felt pretty safe with each other. When Mom and Dad came back, they put the memory foam mattress on the hard bed and tried to sleep. Dad was successful, but Mom tossed and turned all night. It was hard to sleep with them because of that and the hardness of the bed.

The next day, Mom and Dad were gone all day again, and we explored and slept. They came back off and on, bringing things that they had bought. The next day was pretty much the same, except some men brought a big mattress that they put in the bedroom. It was nice and comfortable. Sometimes they really do think of Mina and me. It was very thoughtful of them to buy us such a nice mattress. Mom put sheets, blanket, and comforter on it. Oh, how nice it was! She had a pillow, too. Then Dad brought a small table for the food room, and then a white thing for on top of the counter. Mom said she will cook on that. The man who helped Dad bring things up from the street came back and did something with the washer and the cooker thing. Is this finally home? Mom had her coffee maker and her electric tea kettle and a few frying pans, but how were we to live here without more furniture? Actually, Mina and I had enough for us, but we didn't see how Mom and Dad were going to live with it. Of course, it turned out to be just Mom and us, as Dad left as soon as the man was done with the washer and the cooker thing.

Some men came a few days later and did some things in the food room. They made the heat thing stop leaking and did some things to the food room cabinets. Mom cleaned and cleaned, because there was a lot of dust in the house. She calls it an apartment. She calls it home. It is a house called "polatty." Dad came to visit once and it was really good to see him. We thought maybe he would stay, but he had to go back to his mother's house. Mom says that he will come to live with us when the business is settled, but then he will go to Europe for a while before he is here all the time. Is Europe another house? Why won't he stay here at our house?

Mom has gone out sometimes and has been gone for a whole day sometimes. She says she is teaching English at a school. I'm not sure what English is or, for that matter, what a school is, but if she can teach it, that's fine, as long as she has time for us. Most days she is home with us, but on the weekends she is gone most of the time. She bought some big kettles, and cooked more food for us which, by the way, is very delicious, although Mina doesn't eat it.

The mattress is very comfortable. We usually spend most of the day under the comforter, as this place is not always very warm. There are heat things, but Mom doesn't always turn them on, so it gets cold sometimes. Also, they usually go off at night and Mom has to start them up again in the mornings. It is not a bad place, but the floors are very cold sometimes and make my feet and legs hurt. I sleep in the furry bed a lot, too, not just under the comforter.

Speaking of sleeping, I think I hear a nap calling my name.

Yours,
Apache

Home at Last?

Whee!!! What fun there is here!

We've been here in our new home for some time now, and it's really beginning to feel like home. The floors aren't getting any warmer, but if I run fast enough, it's not too bad. I can really get up some speed running down the hall, and we have been joined here by Ribbon, Mousey, and others. It's great. There is no one here to be scared of Mousey, and Ribbon has been very happy here, too.

The bathroom is different from any bathroom I've ever seen, but it's pretty neat. It is all hard, both the floors and walls. Mom has put our litter box in the bathroom, so now we are almost just like humans. All we need now is to eat at the table, but I don't think that is going to happen. I like to go into the bathroom, even if I don't need the litter box. There is a funny curtain hanging by the shower, which is just part of the floor. I often go into the shower and go around the curtain, since Mom leaves it open on both ends. I can also watch her and Dad take showers. Since it was pretty dusty and dirty at first, here in this new place, Ribbon kept getting dirty, so I took him to the shower and Mom washed him off and hung him outside to dry. Now he is always clean, and I don't have to keep putting him in the water bowl, except when Mom forgets to wash him. I like to go up on the sink, too, and lick the water out of it. I do that in the shower, too. For some reason the water in the bathroom tastes good.

As I mentioned earlier, it is easy to run fast down the hallway. The floor is tile, so things (like Mousey) slide very easily and quickly. He squeaks and squeaks as he speeds down the floor.

What fun! The floors are awfully cold, though, so we spend a lot of time in the bedroom. The floor there is not so cold, because it is not tile. Also, our mattress and comforter are in the bedroom, as well as our furry beds. Miss Patchy sleeps in the furry beds a lot, but I always prefer the big bed. Sometimes I jump up behind the window curtains and look out the window. There are lots of people outside walking around, and lots of cars and trucks. Lots of things to watch! Sometimes small humans play with balls (just like me) and other things. These small humans look pretty much like big humans, just smaller. Miss Patchy is beginning to think that maybe there are baby humans after all. She has not seen much herself, since she is unable to jump up on the window because of her back legs, so I have told her all about it. She has looked down from the balcony and, I think, from the couch room, so she has seen a little bit.

Speaking of the couch room, the door to it is almost always closed. I would love to spend some time in there, but we can go in only when Mom is in there, and then she won't let us get up on the furniture. It is white and kind of furry (I was up on it once) and doesn't look like any other furniture we've ever had. It's funny-shaped and has big pillows on it. I think I could love it a lot. At least the floor in the couch room is not cold, because there is a big rug on the floor. The furniture looks very nice and comfortable and I would love to spend some time on it, but I haven't figured out how to do so without Mom's knowing that I'm doing it. There also is a funny kind of curtain on the window, and I keep getting my claws caught in it. That used to be all there was on the window, but Mom complained that the people across the street could look right in at night, so now there is a big, white curtain behind the funny one. It keeps us from seeing into the windows across the street, so I guess those people can't see in ours, either. Mom likes that, because she is working on a puzzle. I don't know why she likes to do that, as it means sitting in a chair for a long time, looking at little pieces of cardboard. She picks some up and then puts them down, then picks up some more and puts them back down, until once in a while she smiles and says something and puts a piece somewhere else on the table, hooking it to others that are already there. In a way, I like puzzles, too, but I like to pick up the little pieces that are hooked to the others and take them down to the floor to check them out. I don't see anything great about them, but since Mom keeps working with them, I keep trying to figure out what is so great about them. Who can explain why Mom (or any other human) likes certain things?

There is another room in this house, but it is very small, and Dad goes in there a lot by himself. I am almost never allowed to go in there, but I want to check it out. It smells good, and there is a hole in the floor with water in it. Mom keeps the bucket and mop in there, too. It also is all tiled, like the bathroom. Mom calls it a "squatter." I don't know what that means, but Mom says she will not ever use it, except for storing the mop and bucket.

Well, it's getting late, and I have a lot of playing to catch up on, so I will be back later.

Regards,
Mina

Why Do These Things Happen?

Thank goodness it's warm enough for a good nap. I was beginning to think that naps were going to be cold forever.

We have just survived a most terrible time! Last week, I think it was, the lights went out when Mom was getting ready to bake something. She was not happy about that, because, at the same time, the heat went off, too. Anyway, she didn't think much about it, so we didn't, either. Mom thought the lights would be back on fairly soon, but she was terribly wrong! She went to her class, and when she got back, it was still dark and getting very cold in our home, but she didn't turn on the heat. She put on a lot of clothes and after eating a little something, we all went to bed. It wasn't too bad when we were all snuggled up together. Mom put some extra blankets on the bed and she got so warm that she was sweating.

When we got up the next morning, it was colder than ever! How horrible! I hardly felt like eating, because it was so cold. Mom said that Dad couldn't get a train to come home, so it would be at least Monday before we had any lights. I think that was two night times away, so she was not at all happy about it. Mina and I spent all day under the comforter, so we could keep warm. We all snuggled again that night (Mom says it was Saturday night), but the next morning was even colder! I told Mom time and again that I was cold, but she didn't do anything about it. Why didn't she just turn on the heat? Why did Dad have to be here to get lights? There are so many human things that I just do not understand! Anyway, we ate breakfast and spent that day under the comforter, too. That night, we all snuggled together once again to keep warm. It would have been much easier to just turn on the heat!

The next morning, which Mom said was Sunday, it was colder yet and I thought that we all were going to freeze to death. I complained to Mom a lot, but still she did nothing. When she came home from her night class, she brought a stranger upstairs with her and, using a flashlight, put us in the box, and packed up our food and litter box. We all rolled off in the stranger's car to her house. We were let out of the box in a place that had furniture (couches and chairs), lots of plants, and clothes on the drying rack. It was warm! Mom was out with the stranger for a while and then she came in and lay down on the couch and covered up with a comforter. Mina and I let her sleep for a while, but we just had to talk to her about the new place and ask her if we were going to live there now. How many moves can a person make? Anyway, she kept telling us to be quiet and go to sleep, but we just couldn't do it.

In the morning, Mom spent some more time with the stranger and then a man and two boys looked in to see us. Very soon, we were put into the carrier and everything packed up. The stranger dropped us off at our place and left. Mom carried us and everything else up the stairs to our apartment. Oh, it was so cold! We immediately went under the comforter. Mom went out for a little bit that day, but then she got under the covers with us and spent most of the rest of the day there. Finally, after dark, Dad came home. It was warm in our bed that night, with the four of us in it.

In the morning, as soon as he could, Dad left the house and came back quite a while later and said that we would have lights that night. It would be better to have heat! We spent the day under the comforter once again. After dark, the lights suddenly came on and, coincidentally, so did the heat. It has taken a very long time to get warm in here, and it's not really all that warm now, but it's better than it was. Mom and Dad are still cold, but they don't complain too much. Mina and I are not complaining, even though we would like it warmer. At least all four of us are together and able to keep each other warm. Mina and I always have the comforter, although sometimes I do sleep in the furry bed again. It was too cold before, but now I have my heart cushion on my suitcase right next to the radiator and Mina sits on the food room radiator. I'm so glad things are back to normal again. Mom says it will get warmer, but it will just take a little time.

Why did the heat go off at the same time the lights went out? Mina and I could do just fine without lights, but Mom and Dad seem to like them a lot. The heat, however, is a much different matter. We were so cold! How could Mom do that to us? At least she could cook, but that didn't do much for us, only for her. She kept using a candle and a flashlight and she kept boiling water. It felt a little bit warmer in the food room, but nowhere else. Also, why didn't she watch TV or something so we all could have cuddled together to keep warm? Mom is very strange sometimes, always thinking of herself instead of us.

Well, I think the comforter needs me, so I will be off for a nap.

Yours,
Apache

Mom is Getting Smarter

Ribbon is so much fun! We play together so often that I have to take Ribbon into the bathroom so Mom will give him a shower. I like Ribbon to be clean, like me.

Well, Mom is finally starting to realize the beauty of litter, but she's not quite there yet. Whenever she needs to use the bathroom, she always sits on the white thing she calls a toilet. I don't see the point in it, but she always uses it. Dad sometimes uses it, but sometimes he uses the place that Mom calls the Squatter. Anyway, these days, when Mom sits on the white thing, she scratches with her foot in the litter at the same time. Of course, she hasn't learned to use the box yet and just scratches at the litter that is on the floor by the toilet, but she's learning, and that's always encouraging. Every time she goes into the bathroom to use the toilet, I dash in and use the litter box to show her how it is done. One day, maybe she will actually use the box, like she did way back in the summer when we lived one day at a little house. She will be a little big for the box, though, so maybe she will get a bigger one so that all four of us can use it. I'm not sure that Dad will ever learn, though. He just doesn't seem to get it.

Mom also recognizes when the litter box has to be cleaned – not as soon as Miss Patchy and I know it, though. She seems to smell when it is dirty, plus she sees that Miss Patchy and I refuse to use it after a while. I remember when we had no electricity for a while, it was very cold and Miss Patchy and I had to go a lot. Mom cleaned it in the dark one day, with the help of a flashlight. She complained that it was much too wet and that she had just cleaned it, but we couldn't help it. It was the cold that did it.

It's amazing what humans can learn if you have patience and show them enough times how to do things. For instance, I have trained Mom to give Ribbon a shower when he is in the bathroom. I am also trying to train her to get up during the night and play with me. However, she seems to be missing the point. I bang the wardrobe doors together and, when she doesn't respond, I bang even louder. She finally gets up, but instead of playing with me, she goes into the couch room and sleeps on the couch. It is no use banging the doors anymore, because Dad never responds. Anyway, last night I tried, and Mom got up and went into the couch room. However, this time I scratched on the couch room door and meowed, louder and louder, until she finally came out. Unfortunately, she had a trick up her sleeve and she opened all the wardrobe doors. Well, I shut one of them and began to bang it. She got up and used her final trick. She put her purse in the way of the double doors, so I couldn't close either one of them and I couldn't bang them, either. Rats! I'll have to see what else I can do.

Back in the house called Phoenix, there was a wonderful, big chain hanging down the wall in Mom and Dad's bedroom, and I used to pull on it and let it go back against the wall. It made a wonderful loud noise. That really bothered Mom and Dad, and they would get up and shut me out of the bedroom. That made me mad! However, I kept trying, hoping that they would get the idea and come play with me. I thought that the wardrobe doors would be a great substitute for the chain, but no luck. Mom says that I need to be up more during the day, playing, but that just doesn't feel right to me.

Well, I will continue with my training efforts and hope to see some results before long. I am working so hard at it, that it would be a shame if nothing ever came of it. Miss Patchy says to just forget about it and go to sleep, because humans are untrainable. I refuse to give up!

I am feeling as though I need to play, and I see Ribbon on the hall floor, getting cold. Once I have finished playing, I will start to keep track of my training attempts and see how long it takes.

Regards,
Mina

Why Must I Learn Something New?

Lately, it has been very hard to get up from my naps. I would rather just nap all the time and forget about anything else but eating.

However, instead of being allowed to do that, I now have to learn something new. Mom is insisting that I learn to read lips. At least I think that's what it's called. I have no idea why, but she keeps moving her lips just the way she does when she talks, but no sound comes out. It's very frustrating, even though I am beginning to learn some of the things she is saying. I have learned to read Mom's lips when she says: "Patchy, I love you." That's nice to know, but I would love to hear her voice again. She just refuses to make sounds, though. She is even cruel enough that she no longer calls me for supper, so I have to be vigilant about the time, or I might miss my meal. Sometimes I can hear her talk, but very softly; she must forget that she is teaching me to read lips. For some reason, Dad has joined in this cruel behavior, as well. I don't even think that Mom and Dad make sounds to each other anymore, either. I see them moving their lips to each other, but no sound. When I talk, Mom always puts her finger to her lips, telling me to be quiet or to talk more softly. I just don't understand this whole thing. Why are they doing this to me? It's funny, but Mina says she hears them. I think she is just lying to me. How could she hear them and I cannot?

They also sneak up on me all the time. Whenever I have my back turned, I will turn around and there is one of them coming toward me. It makes me jump because I am so startled. Sometimes, I feel the air move when they are passing by, and it really bothers me that they are sneaking up on me. Why are they doing this? Don't they want me to know that they are there? Are they trying to avoid me? So many questions, but no answers.

At least Mom has been cooking some good food lately. The last batch had what Mina said Dad calls Hamsi in it. He brought home a kilo of it. It is very obviously fish and it tasted very good mixed with the chicken, livers, and hearts. Mom is a great cook when she wants to be. Dad cooked some of the Hamsi for himself, too, because I could smell it very strongly. Mina told me that Mom said that Hamsi are little fish that she calls anchovies, and that it made the whole house smell for days and she hated it. I smelled it, too, but I thought it smelled very good and I was sorry when it was gone. Mom didn't eat any. Some people just have no taste. She doesn't eat livers or hearts, either. Very strange! How does Mina know what they are saying? Can she already read lips?

Mom has started something new with me. She hates it when I scratch the rug in the bedroom and it always wakes her up. I thought it would be a good way to get her to wake up and feed me my breakfast early. I guess I was wrong (for the first time ever). Mom now gets up and chases me into the office room and shuts the door. I was pretty mad about it this morning, and left her a little present on the floor. She noticed it right away when she opened the door to let me out for breakfast. I saw her wrinkle her nose. Well, she fed us and then cleaned up the mess. She flushed what she could pick up, then used a wet paper towel, and then mopped with the smelly floor cleaner. When she put the mop away, she stepped on our water dish and flipped it over, getting a lot of water in her slipper and all over the floor. Mom was very angry, but I laughed a lot. That should teach her to lock me up! I hope she isn't thinking of doing it again.

Dad has gone away again. I don't know when he'll be back, as they never tell me anything anymore. I feel so hurt and unloved now that they are not talking to me. Will it ever end?

It is time for a nap now. Writing makes me really, really tired, as does thinking about my problems, so I will say goodbye for now.

Yours,
Apache

Ribbon

Whee!! I love to play! Ribbon makes it so much fun.

Let me tell you something about Ribbon. He is black, with white spots, sort of like me, except I don't really have spots. Mom says I am a tuxedo feline. Whatever! Anyway, Ribbon is long and thin and just has hours and hours of play in him. He also likes to do the things I do. Mom helped me to take some pictures of Ribbon and I am posting them here.

Here is a picture of Ribbon waiting in the hall for me to get up so we can play.

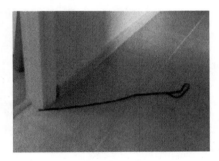

Here is a picture of Ribbon drinking water out of our bowl.

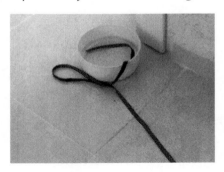

I think I mentioned before that Ribbon likes to take showers, which I don't, but he likes to be clean, like me. Here is a picture of Ribbon waiting for the shower.

This is a picture of Ribbon in the shower. You can't see the water beating down on him, but it is. Believe me, I would not go in there.

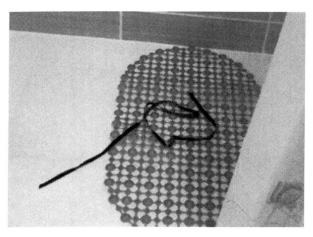

This is a picture of Ribbon drying off. He doesn't use a towel, the way Mom and Dad do, but he dries very quickly. When he is totally dry, I take him down and we play some more.

It's so much fun to have a clean friend to play with. Sometimes he jumps in the air and when Mom or Dad play with us, he jumps really high and I have to leap and twist to get him down.

Well, all this thinking about playing makes me want to go find Ribbon or Mousey and have a good time.

Regards,
Mina

Where is Mom?

I have been napping a lot now. It helps with the loneliness. I'm just tired all the time, and now I'm cold, too.

One day, Mom brought out the suitcases. That is always a bad sign. She put one suitcase inside another one, and then brought out a small one, too. She put some clothes in them and a few other things that she said she was not going to bring back. It was very strange, why two suitcases in one? She said that she was taking one back to the person who owned it. Why was it here if someone else owned it? I sometimes have trouble understanding the human thought process.

Anyway, Mom and Dad left the house one evening with the suitcases and Mom's large purse. It was dark already, and they fed us before they left. I don't know where they went, but they didn't come back. Some strange woman wearing a scarf came into the house and gave us food. Is she Dad's Mother? Mina was scared and hid, but I'm just too tired to hide anymore. I hide only from the vacuum cleaner because it is loud. I can't really hear it now, but I hide when I see it. It is cold now, and the heat does not come on. Mina and I snuggle under the comforter on the bed. Thank goodness for the comfortable mattress and the nice, warm comforter they bought us. We would freeze without them. It is very quiet in the house. Where are they?

A couple of days later, Dad came home, but Mom was not with him. Where is Mom? I fear that she is dead, or she would have come back. She would not leave us if she were alive. Oh, how we miss Mom. At least we have Dad. That is enough for Mina, but to me Dad is someone new in my life. I have lived with Mom for a very long time, long before Dad came into the picture. Don't get me wrong, I love Dad, but I need Mom! I wonder what they have done with her. She has been gone for a long time.

Dad is very good to us. He feeds us and he cleans the litter box. He plays with Mina, and he snuggles with me in the couch room. What more could we ask? I want Mom. We both miss her so much.

A few days later, Dad left again, with that woman coming in to feed us. Now where is Dad? Why did he leave us again? What are we going to do? Maybe Dad is dead, too! It is cold again, quiet, and lonely. Food is definitely okay, but we need Mom and Dad. I am shivering now with cold and fear.

Maybe a good, long nap will help me to feel better. Maybe Mina will cuddle up and help to keep me warm.

Yours,
Apache

Mom's Home!

What a nice nap! It's warm and cozy here, and Mina and I snuggle under our comforter on our wonderful, comfortable mattress.

It was so great to see Mom and Dad. They came home early in the morning and fed us right away. Then we all took a long nap. We were so happy! Mom came home with a lot of suitcases, and they were full of things that she brought from away. One of the things she brought home was treats! Oh, we haven't had any treats for ever so long. They are so delicious! That's our Mom! Always thinking of us, as is only right. Mom had some familiar smells on her, but also some very unfamiliar ones, too. I smelled other felines, but none that I have ever met. I also smelled Mom's daughter and grandson. They weren't in the suitcases, though. I guess maybe they wouldn't fit. It would be nice if they were here, but not their felines. That would be too much.

There were all kinds of other smells, too, some that made me sneeze, Mina, too. Mom brought more of that coffee stuff that she likes to have every morning. I don't know why she likes it, as it smells bad to me. There were no meat smells, so I didn't spend much time sniffing her suitcases. I just want to cuddle and snuggle and let her know how much we missed her. Sometimes we snuggle with Dad in the couch room. That's always nice, because we get to lie on the couches that they bought. When the couches came to the house, we thought that Mom and Dad bought them for us, but we aren't allowed in the couch room unless they are in there. We have to lie on blankets on the couches, which is not bad. I don't especially like the feel of the material on the couches anyway. Dad watches television a lot, so I get to cuddle up next to him, lying on the nice soft blanket. It is so warm and nice. Every time he gets up, I move over to the warm spot he has left. It's funny, but he never appreciates this. Mina always just lies on the other couch and glares at us.

Ever since Mom got back, she has been sleeping a lot. She said something about jet lag. I don't know what it is, but if it makes her snuggle with me in the bed, there is a lot to be said for it. Again, she mentioned flying. What can I do to disabuse her of this delusion? She has no wings, so she cannot fly. Why can't she see that? She said that Mina and I flew, too, some time ago, but we have no wings either. I guess if that's the only thing wrong with Mom (and Dad, too), I can accept it. It kind of bothers me, though. Mina just says that she wishes she could fly, so that maybe she could catch one of those birds that are constantly flying around. She can catch the flies, because they come into the house through the open windows, but the birds never do. Mom keeps telling Mina that the birds are about as big as she is and that she might have trouble catching one, no matter what. Mom says that they are called pigeons, doves, and magpies. Hmmmm! Mom loves to eat pie, but what kind of a pie is a magpie?

Life is almost back to normal now, except that Dad keeps talking about moving to "a stand bull." What is that? Now we are going to live in a bull? A turkey wasn't enough? I will never understand these things, so I might as well go back to sleep and have a nice nap.

Yours,
Apache

Mom Apologized!

A nap is always so refreshing, so I take one as often as possible. Mina says I am just lazy, but she is a lot younger and doesn't seem to need so many naps.

Well, my anger has cooled off now and I can talk about the incident. I was so terribly angry with Mom. I just don't know how she can be so kind and loving sometimes and just so horribly cruel other times. I expressed my anger in no uncertain terms. I would not allow her to touch me and I would not snuggle in bed. I stayed at the foot of the bed and just lay there with my eyes open, just staring into space and looking hurt. Well, I was hurt! My feelings were terribly hurt. What did she do? The unthinkable! When she washed the dishes the other night, she actually closed and latched the food room door! I couldn't get in! How could she do such a thing? And it was just before supper time, to add insult to injury. I called at the door, but she paid no attention. Later on, when she opened the door again, it was all I could do to eat the supper she put in my bowl. I'm hoping she won't do that again, because it is just beyond cruel. Mom has apologized many times and she promises that it won't happen again. We shall see!

I'm happy to report that Mom and Dad sometimes now talk aloud. Only sometimes, though. Mina says the reason I think they aren't talking is because I am going deaf. Hmph! Of all the impertinence of that cheeky, little girl! I don't know why Mom brought her into the house anyway. She says she brought Mina home for me. Why on earth she would do that is beyond me. Anyway, sometimes I can hear them talking and can even hear the muzin once in a while. It's nice to hear their voices; I just wish they would keep on talking and not mouth what they are saying. It's so rude! Deaf, indeed!

Mom now leaves the balcony door open a lot. I don't actually go out, but I often sit in the doorway, enjoying the breeze or the little bit of sun that comes there in the afternoon. I don't dare go all the way out, with Mom's penchant for closing doors. I could get stuck out there! Mina says it's fun out there, but I'll just let her have that kind of fun. It's all cold floor, with nothing soft to lie on, so I'll just stick with the inside where I have lots of options. She also opens the bedroom window a lot now, but leaves the see-through curtain over the opening. She says it keeps out birds and flies.

We had some very loud rain last night. There was a lot of what Mom and Dad call thunder and lightning. It got so loud that it was scary. Mom gave a little scream at one point, because she said the lightning must have hit something. It was a very loud crack! She hasn't yet been able to find out what, if anything, was hit by the lightning. I don't like that kind of rain, but Mina says it is much louder than I think, because I just can't hear it all that well.

Mom and Dad got some really good food in a can. They say it is beef. That's fine with me, as it is very delicious. Even Mina likes it. Mom says that Mina's problem is that she likes only red meat, and not chicken. We had a can of lamb and kidney before and Mina liked that, too. Mom says she will get a can once in a while.

Talking about Mom screaming, she also growls. She growls a lot. They are just short little growls and come on at any time, whether she's angry or not. I don't understand these little growls. Why does she do it? Sometimes there will be a lot of them all at once, and sometimes they are very loud. Often, she holds her stomach after growling. I don't know what her stomach has to do with anything. Maybe her mind is going and in her confused state she thinks there is something to growl at. Oh well, just one more human mystery not to understand.

Well, all this thinking has made me very tired, so I'm going to have to take a nap. Maybe in a dream the answer to why Mom growls will come to me.

Yours,
Apache

Life Must Go On

I haven't felt much like playing lately; in fact, I've been a little depressed.

Miss Patchy and I have been talking, and we are certain that Dad is dead. We have not seen him since the really hot weather, and why would he be gone so long if he was still alive? Mom says he will be home soon, but we think she is just deluding herself. I guess it's time to get busy with life and continue on, even though we will miss Dad a lot. He always brushed Miss Patchy and gave us both treats. He spent quite a bit of time in the couch room, our favorite room. It is closed most of the time now, because Mom doesn't spend much time there. She was going in there just about every night to watch some TV, but now she says that she can't get the TV to work, so she just opens the door for a while and lets us go in there. It's not much fun without either her or Dad. Mom says that Dad would have been home sooner, but his nephew, the one we like, had to go to the hospital and have surgery. A likely story. We know he's dead.

I was very upset for a few days. A while ago, Mom invited me up onto her lap while she was sitting at the computer, as she usually does. This time, I'm not sure what happened, but I jumped up onto her lap and was just getting around to hugging her when she jumped and yelled at me. I turned and jumped down onto the floor and she yelled at me some more. Something about scratching her. Later that night, she had the bedroom curtains closed over the windows, but something was showing on the curtain. I could see it in the light coming through from the outside. I wanted to see what it was, so I jumped up at it and grabbed onto the curtains with my claws so I could climb up. Mom yelled at me again, and I jumped down. Twice she called me a bad girl! Twice! I was so crushed and hurt! For a few days I didn't eat anything that she gave me and I spent all day sleeping on the bed or in the wardrobe. I wanted to just die and not bother her any more.

Since that time, Mom has made a point of coming to me every time she comes into the bedroom. She pets me and tells me what a good girl I am, what a pretty girl I am. She also says she is sorry for yelling at me, but that I punctured her leg and scratched her tummy, and it surprised her and hurt. Also, she said I ripped the bottom trim off part of the curtain and now she will have to take it down to repair it. She says it's not a bad tear, as the curtain itself is not torn, just the trim came off. I am glad to hear that, but I still feel a little bad. I've started to eat again, though, and I still go up on her lap, but I am very careful now. She and I take a nap together almost every day, and the three of us usually sleep together at night. There is plenty of room on the bed, now that Dad is no longer here.

It's cold these days, and it's very confusing, because Mom keeps the windows closed most of the time now. We don't think it's all that cold, but Mom does. She is wearing warmer clothes now and is using the heavy, red blanket now at night. That is our favorite blanket, because it's so soft and cuddly. Mom said she thought that when it got cold, the young humans would stay inside, but she guesses it is not yet cold enough, because they are still out playing and screaming all day and into the night. However, it's not as late as before. They seem to go in around the time it gets dark now. Mom is grateful for that. Most nights these days, the bedroom window is closed, so it gets very quiet.

Mom has started drying the clothes inside. I think she did that before when it was cold and the windows were all closed. She says if it gets sunny and warm again for a while, she will move the drying rack outside, but for now it is in the office with wet clothes on it. Now there is less room to play in there.

Well, I'm going to take a look for Ribbon and see if he feels like playing. I'm not sure I do, but I guess I should try. Even Miss Patchy has been playing a little now. Mom is very surprised by that, because Miss Patchy is old and sleeps most of the time. Almost every day now, she plays with the green rat with the bell on it.

I see Ribbon, but he says he doesn't feel like playing. I guess maybe I will take a nap.

Regards,
Mina

Strange Days

I am beginning to feel a little more like playing lately. It has been hard to know exactly how I feel. One day, Dad is here, the next day he's not. He has now been gone for quite a while, so we are pretty sure he is dead. Mom keeps saying he will be gone longer, but will be back, and will bring some treats for us. Ha! I hardly remember treats. Mom says they are too expensive here, wherever here is. Miss Patchy says that we are in a turkey. Ha! I think we ate a turkey once!

Speaking of Miss Patchy, Mom is an apologist for her. She sleeps most of the time and often gets very cross when I want to play with her. Sometimes I attack her just to make her show a reaction. Well, of course she growls and hisses; that's natural. But Mom gets upset about it and tells me to stop. Anyway, Miss Patchy plays with the toys every now and then, which is what she is doing today. She's been playing with the green mouse that has a little bell on it. Mom loves it when Miss Patchy plays with the toys. All the time, when Miss Patchy is sleeping, or being cross with me, Mom keeps telling me that Miss Patchy is old and we need to be nice to her. Ha! She is old, all right! Sometimes she almost falls over when she is on the bed, and she even needs to have a box by the bed in order to get on it, because she can no longer jump. A lot of times, Miss Patchy goes into a room or gets up on the bed and just stands there for a minute, looking around, trying to figure out where she is and why she is there. That's old!

I, on the other hand, am young and healthy. I'm a pretty girl and a good girl, also a smart girl. Mom tells me this all the time. Of course, she tells the same things to Miss Patchy, too, but I know it's true for me. I always try to do the right things. However, when I occasionally forget myself, I feel so terrible when Mom tells me that I was wrong. She never hits me or even calls me a "bad girl," so it's not real bad, but maybe I feel even worse because of it. I want to be good and I want her to love me all the time. It's so nice when she lets me come up on her lap and I reach up and hug her around the neck and knead. Sometimes I kiss her, too. Mom says she loves it.

This morning, Mom and I were on the chair in front of the computer. We were hugging. Suddenly that skinny little box that Mom talks to sometimes, began to call out. Mom immediately dumped me on the floor and ran into the food room to the box. She talked to the box and then she held it out to me, saying that it was Daddy. Right! Daddy is not a box, and he is much too big to fit inside the box. The box sounded like Daddy, but you can't fool me. It wasn't him. It would be nice to see him again and hear his voice for real, but as Mom says: "I'm not going to hold my breath." That seems like a funny thing to say. How can you hold your breath? You can't even see it, let alone get hold of it. Mom has very funny ideas sometimes.

Today, as soon as she fed Miss Patchy and me, Mom took the bed apart and put the sheets in that funny, spinning thing in the food room. I hate it when she does that, because the blankets are all lumped up on the bed, and it's not easy to find a comfortable spot. Miss Patchy doesn't like it, either. Of course, she mostly lies on the suitcase by the radiator in Mom's office, unless Mom is in the bed. Sometimes I will lie on the suitcase with her, because it is nice and warm there. When Mom watches TV, which she does almost every night, Miss Patchy hogs the place by Mom on the couch. I just lie on the other couch and glare at Mom. She tries to get me to come over to her and share the couch with her and Miss Patchy, but I don't want to share. I want Mom to come over to my couch! I am *very disappointed when she doesn't come. Once in a while she will come to sit with me, but she tells me that the other couch is better for her because it is easier for her to see the TV from it. Sometimes I think she just loves Miss Patchy more than she loves me.*

Both Miss Patchy and I keep begging for treats. Sometimes Mom will cook chicken or a hamburger and will offer us pieces of it. Miss Patchy loves it all, but I just won't eat it. I did eat a piece of raw hamburger once, but I don't like it cooked. Miss Patchy will eat just about anything, except yesterday Mom cooked what she calls a "wiener." She put a small piece of it on the floor for Miss Patchy, but she wouldn't eat it. That was a surprise. It surprised Mom, too.

Almost every morning I have been asking to go outside on the balcony. Every morning, it seems colder and colder out there. Mom always shuts the door when I go out, so I have to call her or scratch on the door to get her attention when I want to come in. I didn't bother this morning. It's just too cold. Why does that happen? Before, it was very warm, and sometimes quite hot, on the balcony. Now my feet freeze when I go out there on the tiles. Once when I went out there was some white stuff on the balcony floor and it was very cold. Miss Patchy and Mom said it is snow. So that is snow! I don't think I like it. Mom always tries to be close when I go out, because she doesn't want me to get too cold. Sometimes she will pick me up and cuddle me tightly, trying to warm up my cold fur. She really is a good Mom.

One time, when the balcony was warm, I was out on it, a bird came and sat on the railing, and it was looking me over very thoroughly. It was pretty big, and there was another one up on the balcony roof. Mom said they were magpies and were probably eyeing me as a possible meal. She brought me in right away and shooed those nasty birds away. I have often thought of eating birds, as we do eat turkey, which is a bird, but I never thought that a bird could eat a feline! That is kind of scary. I will now watch out for birds.

This morning the doorbell rang. I hate when that happens. Miss Patchy is lucky, because there is a lot that she no longer can hear, but I think her hearing is better now than it was for a while. I always hide when I hear the doorbell, and Miss Patchy hides, too, when she realizes that it has rung. Anyway, Mom answered the door and someone handed her one of those things she calls a bucket. She went into the bathroom and filled it with water and handed it back out the door. Then the doorbell rang again, and it was the same person. This time, Mom gave her a small piece of paper. I'm hoping that they are done ringing the doorbell!

Well, I don't feel so much like playing right now, so I think I will take a nap in the wardrobe. It's a nice quiet spot, with no breezes.

Regards,
Mina

The New Normal

Well, we lived in the turkey for quite some time. Mom says it was three years. We never got to know any of the felines who lived outside in the neighborhood. I guess they were busy living and didn't have time for us. They said that we were spoiled and just were not their kind. So, as Mom would say: "Their loss!"

You may think that this looks like Miss Patchy's writing, but it is me, Mina. I will try to catch you up on the long time it has been since my last post. Our life was pretty good while we were in the turkey, but some say that "all good things must come to an end." I think they may be right.

One day, Mom and Dad began to put things in boxes. Oh-oh! I've seen that before, and it never means good things. Miss Patchy agreed with me. She said it was never a good sign when they started putting things in suitcases and boxes. They also packed a lot of clothes in the two big suitcases. It made me afraid. I was right to be afraid, although that part of life is over and I now must go on. Dad had been gone for most of the time we lived in the turkey. We missed him a lot, but it didn't seem to matter to him. He was always good to us when he was home, but it just was not very often. Mom cooked a lot of things, including our food made with chicken. I won't eat it, but Miss Patchy loved it. Mom found some really good litter there, and things were quite odorless.

To get back to my update: one day, Dad's brother, Memmet, came, and he spent the night. The next morning, both Miss Patchy and I were put into one box and we and the suitcases were taken out to a car. Oh no, here we go again! Memmet was driving and Dad sat in the front seat and Mom was in the back with us. We drove for a long time, and then we were in a big place with people running around everywhere. It was noisy, and neither I nor Miss Patchy liked it. Mom said it was an airport in "a car a." Finally, after sitting around for a long time, we walked down a long hall, and went outside and got into some sort of big thing (Mom called it an airplane). There were lots of seats in the thing and Mom and Dad sat in two of them and we (in one box) and the computer sat with them. There were a lot of people and a lot of different smells. Every now and then, a stranger would look at us and say something to Mom and Dad. Usually, I think they were admiring us and that made us proud. The thing we were in seemed to begin to move and roar and then it got very light-feeling, and it got a little quieter, except that there was a sort of whistling sound along with the roar. We were in the thing for a while and then it began to roar again and there were some clunking noises from beneath our box, and then a big bump. It was a little scary, since we had no idea what was going on. Mom said that the airplane was flying, and we were flying with it. More of her delusions!

We got out of the thing then, and went into a very big place where there were a lot of people. They were everywhere! Mom said it was in the airport in a stand bull. It took a while, standing in lines, but then we were running down a hall. Dad dropped our box a couple of times, but he continued to run after picking us up. We finally stopped running and we all piled into another big thing with lots of seats. Again, we were there with Mom and Dad and people admired us. More roaring and more light-feeling and whistling. Once again the roars and clunking, a big bump, and we got out of the thing. Mom said we were in an airplane, both times, and that we had one more to go. She said that we were in "Switz." Let me tell you that airports are big and noisy and certainly would not be nice places to live!

The third airplane was the biggest of all, and we were looked at by lots of people and some of those people kept asking if we needed anything. They were very nice, but we were safe in our box, keeping each other company. Miss Patchy was not happy about any of it. She had not been feeling very good for some time, and these airplanes were very hard on her. More roaring and light-feeling. We stayed for a very long time in the third airplane until there was more roaring and clunking, a big bump, and then we got out and into another airport. We had to stand in line for a while until some people asked Mom and Dad questions. Then we went to another place and answered some questions. Finally, we went out into the air. It was dark, and the place smelled somehow familiar, as though we had been there before, maybe a long time ago.

We got into another big thing that Mom called a bus. Lots of seats and our box was put up on a seat so everyone could see us and admire us. We didn't cry at all, the whole time, but we were really happy to get out of that bus. Then we were loaded into a car! In the car was Linda, Mom's daughter. It was nice to see her again, as it had been some time. We drove for a while and then we got out of the car and went into a familiar-smelling house, but some different feline smells, too. Miss Patchy was happy to say that she did not detect the odor of the nasty Mr. Purr. In fact, she did not smell any of the felines who were there before, but there were plenty of new smells.

We went up to two rooms and we were let out of our box. It was familiar, but still a little scary. The second room was where we'd had a hiding place when we had been there before, and we looked and looked for it, but it was gone. Miss Patchy went downstairs a few times and told me that the new felines treated her with great respect. One time, she went up on a couch and sat next to Mom. She told me that there were four felines downstairs – a gray one called Spencer, two orange brothers called Felix and Sammy, and a black female named Holly. Based on her word, I tried going downstairs a few times, but gray Spencer came up the stairs and began to hiss and growl at me. I hissed and growled back, but we never actually got into a fight. He ran back downstairs and I ran back up and into our rooms. Almost every night, someone would try to come upstairs, but I always chased them back down. They never once treated me with respect! I guess that is only for old people.

There is also a feline who lives upstairs, but in Linda's room. Her name is Maya and she has an awful lot of fur! When she lived with someone else, they used to shave her every summer. She must have looked really funny. I think I would laugh at her if I saw that.

Well, Ribbon is here, and so is mousey, so I need to go play with them now.

Regards,
Mina

More New Normal

We have been in this house for some time now, because Mom says she can't afford to move. Recently, Dad went away and we haven't seen him since. Maybe he is really dead now. We miss him a lot, but I don't think he's coming back. He took all his things and walked out the door. Mom said that he moved out and that they are getting a divorce. I guess that means we won't see him again. What more can happen to us?

Another big change was when Mom and Dad took Miss Patchy downstairs, but never brought her back. I fear that she is dead, too. As nasty as she was to me at first, we had grown close. She was a little like a mother to me, and I actually miss her. It is very boring here with both Mom gone much of every day and Dad gone, maybe forever. Mom keeps telling me that I need to go downstairs and make friends, but I think she just doesn't understand how impossible that is. I have spoken to Maya a few times. She lives in Linda's bedroom and almost never comes out. She is very quiet and never says much. Maybe someday we can be friends, but that may take a while. We always hiss and growl and spit at each other when she is out of Linda's room, and I usually chase her back.

At least Ribbon and Mousey are still the same, but sometimes I can't find them. However, a new toy has entered my life. Mom says that it is called a Cat Dancer, and I just love it, probably more than any other toy I ever had. It jumps and swings and I'm never quite sure which way it will move.

I leap and pounce. Sometimes I just lie there watching it until I am fairly certain of catching it, then I jump on it and maybe catch it. Once in a while it can't get away and I hold onto it and bite at it.

Well, enough for now. Mom played with me this morning and, after all this typing, my paws are aching and I'm tired. I think it's nap time.

Regards,
Mina

Now We are Just One

Miss Patchy has been gone for a very long time now, so I have given up hope of ever seeing her again. Mom says that she has crossed the Rainbow Bridge. I'm not sure where that is, but Mom seems to think that Miss Patchy is happy and healthy again. I miss her. I am also a bit confused. Miss Patchy, where are you? Will you come back to play with me and teach me things? I'm sorry I was jealous of you and didn't always appreciate you. I will promise to be good to you if you will just come back. Mom says that you are healthy and happy now, so we could play together a lot. Just please come back. I'm lonely.

Mom now plays with me nearly every morning and sometimes at night, too. However, it is still pretty boring here. Almost every day Mom goes away for a while, and once she brought someone up to our rooms to meet me. I did not feel like meeting another human, especially a male human. I have smelled him in the house a few times since then, but he has never come upstairs again.

So, life goes on and on. Mom keeps talking about making more money. She says that she lives on Social Security and it is not enough. She wants to be able to move out on her (our) own, but doesn't know how she can ever afford it. I really don't want to move again, but if I just had Mom, my toys, and a long hallway . . .

Endnotes

Page 28 – "chase"   She means a "Chaise."

Page 144 – "Apple Still"   This is an Apostille, a super notary that is accepted internationally.

Page 144 – "con"   She means the Turkish Consulate in Boston

Page 151 - "beljum, luxburg, frans, switz, itali"   She means Belgium, Luxembourg, France, Switzerland, and Italy.

Page 152 – "grease" - Obviously, she means Greece

Page 153 – "Alanya" is a beach resort on the Turkish Riviera, on the Mediterranean.

Page 154 – "Muzin"   She means muezzin, the one who calls out from each mosque the times for prayer five times a day.

Page 161 - "tandir"   This is a clay oven set into the ground in which things are cooked. Similar to the Indian tandoor.

Page 163 – "Ramazan" is the Turkish word for the Arabic Ramadan. It is an important Muslim month.

Page 163 – "Memmet" is actually the name Mehmet, which is a common man's name in Turkey.

Page 163 - In Islam, during Ramazan/Ramadan, people must eat before sunrise and after sunset. Therefore, they get up while it is still dark and cook a big meal to eat before it gets light.

Page 177 – "Polatty" is actually Polatlı, which is a town near Ankara, Turkey.

Page 184 – "Squatter"   This was the term used by Mom to designate the Turkish toilet, nothing more than a hole in the floor surrounded by porcelain, and containing water. Used as a toilet in many parts of the world. A woman must squat to use it for all functions.

Page 196 – "a stand bull"   This, of course, is Istanbul.

Page 208 - "a car a"   is Ankara

Page 209 – "Switz"   is Switzerland

72990128R00119

Made in the USA
Middletown, DE
10 May 2018